Twayne's United States Authors Series

Sylvia E. Bowman, *Editor*

INDIANA UNIVERSITY

Constance Fenimore Woolson

CONSTANCE FENIMORE WOOLSON

by RAYBURN S. MOORE
University of Georgia

TUSAS 34

Twayne Publishers, Inc. New York

Library of Congress Catalog Card Number: 62-19478

MANUFACTURED IN THE UNITED STATES OF AMERICA BY
UNITED PRINTING SERVICES, INC.
NEW HAVEN, CONN.

FOR MARGARET

Preface

THIS VOLUME, a short critical study of Constance Fenimore Woolson, is also something of an introduction to Miss Woolson's work. It begins with a sketch of her life and continues with chapters on her short stories, her novels, her views of fiction in relation to her practice, and her literary reputation. I have discussed neither her poetry nor her descriptive sketches, except incidentally. One may find these aspects of her contribution treated in John D. Kern's *Constance Fenimore Woolson: Literary Pioneer* (1934).

Aside from its approach and treatment of materials, my study differs from that of Kern in another way. I have tried to examine Constance Woolson's work first in relation to her own times and then in the light of ours. Moreover, I have sought to characterize Miss Woolson's contributions to certain currents in late nineteenth-century fiction—especially to the international theme and to the novel of analysis—without neglecting her importance as a writer of local-color fiction.

The foregoing paragraphs were written in January, 1962, when this study was completed. In November the second and third volumes of Leon Edel's biography of Henry James appeared: *The Conquest of London: 1870-1881* and *The Middle Years: 1882-1895*. My manuscript was in proof before I had access to these volumes, and I have therefore not used them in this book. Since, however, Mr. Edel deals extensively with the Woolson-James relationship (especially in *The Middle Years*), some brief comment seems in order.

I shall confine my remarks to three matters: (1) the intimacy of the personal relationship between Miss Woolson and James; (2) Miss Woolson's death; and (3) the quality of Miss Woolson's work.

In regard to the Woolson-James relationship, Mr. Edel seeks to establish a case for a "virtuous attachment" between the two artists and to suggest that Miss Woolson was probably the aggressor in this romance. But documentary evidence for any accurate or thorough treatment of the friendship is limited, as

Mr. Edel admits (he bases his discussion chiefly on four long letters Miss Woolson wrote to Henry James and on interpretations of particular works by both writers). Nevertheless, he offers the fullest account of this relationship yet attempted, though I, for one, have some reservations regarding Constance Woolson's role in this matter.

Secondly, Mr. Edel appears to take it for granted (after an introductory caveat) that Miss Woolson committed suicide. He has every right to this opinion because James thought so, too, but James was not in Venice when Miss Woolson died nor had he, so far as one knows now, any special information that would clearly establish his friend's death as suicide. James's views certainly warrant respect and careful consideration, but I do not think they prove that Constance Woolson took her own life. It seems to me that the facts surrounding this tragic death provide insufficient evidence for any authoritative judgment except, perhaps, the old Scottish verdict of not proven.

Finally, Mr. Edel offers some rather unfavorable critical opinions about Miss Woolson's work. In this regard, however, one need say little since Henry James himself long ago pointed out the virtues of her fiction, and other critics—especially Stedman and Howells in her own day and Pattee, Quinn, Richardson, Brooks, Cowie, and Hubbell in the twentieth century—have discussed her contribution to literature quite favorably.

I have also found much to admire in Constance Fenimore Woolson. I sincerely respect the standards of integrity she set for herself both as person and as artist, and I believe that she contributed something of value to American writing in the last quarter of the nineteenth century. Yet I have neither indiscriminately praised Miss Woolson's fiction nor failed, I trust, to point out its limitations. If my study informs readers of the measure of her achievement and encourages them to seek out for themselves her better novels and stories, it will have served its chief purpose.

R. S. M.

Athens, Georgia

Acknowledgments

It is a pleasure to record here my debt to those who helped me in the preparation of this book. The late Clare Benedict, Constance Woolson's niece, despite ill health in the last year of her life, graciously helped me in many ways; and Mrs. Robert H. Bishop, Jr., Miss Woolson's grandniece, has also been very kind. Miss Katharine Shedd, Miss Benedict's friend, thoughtfully corresponded with me when Miss Benedict was too ill to write herself; and Mr. Philip R. Mather assisted me in the early stages of this study of his grandaunt's work. Mr. Clifton Waller Barrett generously provided me with photostats of five letters written by Miss Woolson. Dr. Lyon N. Richardson not only helped me himself but also urged others to lend their assistance. Dr. Jay B. Hubbell, my teacher and friend, and Dr. Edd Winfield Parks and Dean John O. Eidson, my colleagues, have read my manuscript and offered valuable comments and suggestions. Dr. Sylvia E. Bowman, editor of TUSAS, has also read my typescript to its advantage.

I am grateful to Dean Eidson, Dr. Edwin M. Everett, Dr. Robert A. McRorie, and the Graduate School of the University of Georgia for making it possible for me to devote my full time to this study during the summers of 1960 and 1961. The members of the staff at the University of Georgia Library have been unfailingly courteous, and Mr. W. Porter Kellam, Mr. John D. Marshall, and Mrs. Christine G. Burroughs have been especially helpful. Finally, my most generous creditor is mentioned in the dedication.

I wish to thank the following editors and publishers for permission to quote from their publications:

To Miss Clare Benedict for passages from her *Five Generations;* to the American Book Company for passages from Alexander Cowie's *The Rise of the American Novel* (1948); to Appleton-Century-Crofts, Inc. for passages from Arthur Hobson Quinn's *American Fiction* (1936); to the Duke University Press for passages from Jay B. Hubbell's *The South in American Literature* (1954) and to the editors of the *South Atlantic Quarterly* for passages from articles by Fred Lewis Pattee and Lyon N. Richardson; to E. P. Dutton & Co., Inc. for passages from Van Wyck Brook's *The Times of Melville and Whitman* (1947); to Harper and Brothers for passages from the novels and volumes of short stories by Miss Woolson; to Holt, Rinehart and Winston, Inc. for passages from Edward Wagenknecht's *Cavalcade of the American Novel* (1952); to the editors of the *New England Quarterly* and to Jay B. Hubbell for passages from an article by Dr. Hubbell; to the University of Pennsylvania Press for passages from John D. Kern's *Constance Fenimore Woolson* (1934); and to the editors of the *Saturday Review* for passages from a letter published by John Hervey.

For permission to quote from manuscript materials in their holdings, I should like to thank the librarians and curators of special collections at Butler Library, Columbia University (Mr. Roland Baughman); the Cornell University Library (Mr. John Foote Guido); the Duke University Library (Miss Mattie Russell); Houghton Library, Harvard University (Mr. William A. Jackson); the Western Reserve Historical Society (Mrs. Alene Lowe White); and the Yale University Library (Mr. David R. Watkins).

I am also indebted to Mrs. Robert H. Bishop, Jr., of Chagrin Falls, Ohio, for permission to quote from the manuscripts of the letters Miss Woolson wrote Samuel Mather.

Contents

Chronology

1840	Constance Fenimore Woolson born in Claremont, New Hampshire, March 5.
1840-1841	Winter: Woolson family moves to Cleveland, Ohio, where Constance attends Miss Hayden's School during 1840's.
1850's	Attends Cleveland Female Seminary.
1855	Takes first of several summer voyages to Mackinac Island.
1858	Graduates at head of class from Madame Chegaray's "fashionable New York school."
1861-1865	Contributes to war effort in various ways and shows herself a fervent patriot in the Union cause.
1869	Charles Jarvis Woolson, her father, dies in August.
1870	National magazines publish her first articles and sketches.
1870-1871	Visits New York City and writes articles for the *Supplement* of the *Daily Cleveland Herald.*
1871-1873	Visits relatives in New York and publishes more descriptive sketches and stories in the magazines. *The Old Stone House* (1872), first book, a juvenile, wins prize; published under pseudonym of Anne March.
1873-1879	Autumn, 1873, leaves with mother and sister (Clara W. Benedict) for first trip south. Spends winter of each year in Florida (usually in St. Augustine) with mother and sometimes with Mrs. Benedict. On occasion visits Virginia, the Carolinas, Tennessee, and Georgia. After death of Mrs. Woolson in February, 1879, Miss Woolson leaves South and sails in November for Europe. First book for adults published during this period: *Castle Nowhere: Lake-Country Sketches* (1875).
1880-1883	Lives chiefly in Florence, Venice, and Rome during winter months and in Switzerland or Germany during hot months of summer. *Rodman the Keeper: Southern Sketches* (1880) brought out by D. Appleton in New York. First installment

of *Anne* appears in *Harper's New Monthly Magazine*, December, 1880; book publication follows in 1882. Friendship with Henry James dates from cordial exchange of courtesies in Florence, spring of 1880. *For the Major*, 1883.

1883-1886 Lives in England (chiefly in London and Warwickshire) from autumn, 1883, until spring, 1886. Sees James occasionally and carries on correspondence with him. *East Angels* appears first as serial in *Harper's*; as a book in 1886.

1887-1889 Leases "Villa Brichieri" in Florence from January 1, 1887, until fall of 1889. *Jupiter Lights* published in *Harper's* as serial and as book in 1889. Leaves for trip to Greece late in 1889.

1890-1891 Visits Egypt. Lives in Cheltenham, Gloucestershire, from late spring of 1890 to August of 1891. Works on *Horace Chase.*

1891-1893 Lives in Oxford, works on novel, and sees James frequently. On return trip to Italy in summer of 1893, Miss Woolson contracts influenza in London.

1893-1894 Lives in Venice. *Horace Chase* appears first in *Harper's* and in book form in 1894. In January, 1894, Miss Woolson contracts influenza for second time and dies on January 24, the circumstances of her death being difficult to determine with exactness. James assists Mrs. Benedict in disposition of personal effects.

1895-1896 Harper and Brothers brings out two volumes of stories and one of travel sketches: *The Front Yard and Other Italian Stories* (1895); *Dorothy and Other Italian Stories* (1896); and *Mentone, Cairo, and Corfu* (1896).

Constance Fenimore Woolson

CHAPTER *1*

American Pilgrim at Home and Abroad: A Biographical Sketch

ON October 12, 1889, a writer in the *Critic* pointed out one of the chief problems that writers dealing with Constance Fenimore Woolson's life have confronted: She is not, he stated, "one of the authors who furnish matter for the pens of the paragraph writers. Little is known of her personality. . . ." And the point is well taken even though the writer goes on to describe a brief biographical sketch of Miss Woolson prepared by Arthur Stedman for the October issue of the *Book Buyer*. Stedman's essay notwithstanding, little happened to change this situation during the next forty years; and, in the introduction to her *Constance Fenimore Woolson* (1930), Miss Clare Benedict could still remark without fear of contradiction that the "materials" for a biography of her aunt were "entirely lacking." Much the same thing might be said today, though several articles of a biographical and critical nature have been published in the interim,[1] and John D. Kern's *Constance Fenimore Woolson: Literary Pioneer* (1934) has appeared, not to mention Miss Benedict's own indispensable volumes on Miss Woolson and other members of the family. This lack of a full-scale biography almost seventy years after her death would doubtless please Miss Woolson; for, as a "solitary sort of old bird," she never cared to have her name bruited about—not even in the literary magazines of her own day.

Nevertheless, despite this reticence and the lack of materials, the main facts of Constance Woolson's life are known. One regrets the paucity of documentary evidence concerning her personal and literary relationship with Henry James and one would certainly like to know more about her tragic death, but, aside from these problems, the outline of her literary career and the profile of her personality are reasonably clear.

I *The Pilgrim at Home: Early Life in Cleveland and New York*

Constance Fenimore Woolson (Connie to her family and friends) was born on March 5, 1840, in Claremont, New Hampshire, the sixth child of Charles Jarvis and Hannah Cooper Pomeroy Woolson.[2] C. J. Woolson was a native of Vermont who lived in New York, Boston, and New Hampshire and had engaged at one time or another in the publishing business and journalism, although upon his marriage he entered into the manufacturing of stoves with his father in Claremont. Mrs. Woolson was the daughter of Ann Cooper Pomeroy, one of James Fenimore Cooper's older sisters.[3] A few weeks after the birth of Constance, three of her sisters died of scarlet fever, and before a year had passed, the bereaved family moved to Cleveland, Ohio, in the Western Reserve, where other New Englanders had settled and where Mr. Woolson once again established himself in business.[4]

Cleveland in the 1840's was a town "delightfully situated," according to Mrs. Woolson, on a "bluff." It possessed a history that went back to 1796, when Moses Cleaveland, an agent for the Connecticut Land Company, laid out the town. In the 1840's Cleveland was not yet a railhead nor an industrial city where Lake Superior iron ore could be smelted on a large scale in furnaces with Pennsylvania and western Virginia coal. It had been chartered as a city in 1836, but in some ways it still resembled a country village. In 1840 its 6,000 inhabitants got their water from "their own wells and cisterns," used "outside toilets" because there were no waterworks or sewage systems, and "threw their garbage on the back ash heap or on a collective dump where the village pigs still rooted."[5] Despite its character in 1840, Cleveland was destined for bigger things (2,000 ships a year were already using the little lake port and the Ohio canal had opened up the hinterlands to the town's commercial interests); it began to grow rapidly in the same decade that found the Woolsons arriving from New England.

Thus Constance Woolson grew up in a town that was growing up too, and by the time she had gone to Miss Hayden's school and then to the Cleveland Female Seminary, Cleveland's population had more than trebled. Reacting against her environment, the youthful Constance once wrote a friend that she would "like to go to boarding school very much. I always liked," she observed, "the idea of going away from home for a time" (Benedict, II, 15). A few years later, when her friend Flora Payne was traveling in Europe, Constance commented: "Well, Flo, this is a stupid letter, but what can one say of this stupid place to a person visiting the fairest corners of the earth?" (Benedict, II, 17). And even later, after she had left Cleveland for good, she wrote one of her correspondents: "Cleveland is so large now. . . . I have not been there for more than a year and a half, nor do I expect to return. My dear Father's death broke up our home, and now I am traveling with my Mother. . . . The variety is pleasant after so many years on the monotonous shores of Lake Erie."[6]

Not much is known of Constance Woolson's girlhood, though a general account of her activities may be pieced together by a careful reading of Miss Benedict's volumes, Miss Woolson's own works (especially her book for children, *The Old Stone House,* 1872), and her published and unpublished letters. Lyon N. Richardson has described this period on the basis of a reading of the juvenile book and of some unpublished letters:

> There were paintings and music, and there was literature especially, to interest the children. In one scene in the book, the children, organizing themselves for play, willingly yield the delight of a torchlight procession to play 'Editor's Sanctum,' each child supplying a poem, a story, or an essay. On another occasion they celebrate the Fourth of July with a drama of their own composition, featuring Israel Putnam as hero, the spy Nathan Hale as the villain, and Bunker Hill as a scene of glorious action. Literary expression was a normal part of Miss Woolson's childhood activities.[7]

During this period Constance did her first "original writing," a poem in "imitation" of the style of *Hiawatha.* "It was," she wrote her nephew Samuel Mather many years later, "for a little ms. newspaper which we amused ourselves with one summer [at Mackinac Island]."[8]

As a girl, Constance attended Miss Hayden's School and accompanied her father on trips in the summer to Wisconsin (he owned some property in Milwaukee and Mrs. Woolson had relatives in the state) and to the Zoarite community in the Tuscarawas Valley of Ohio.[9] In the 1850's she attended the Cleveland Female Seminary, which was under the direction of Dr. Samuel St. John, professor of geology at Western Reserve University. There she came to know and admire one of her teachers, Miss Linda Guilford, who had come to Cleveland in 1848 from the recently established Mount Holyoke College in Massachusetts. In several letters written to her old teacher in the 1880's and 1890's, Miss Woolson recalled some of her experiences at the Seminary:

> As I think of all this, a vision arises before me of the 'Cleveland Seminary'—with its furnace-heated air; its crowds of girls, the woods with their early spring flowers, and you, and Prof. St. John, and Miss Barstow taking charge of us all. I see the snow as it used to drive slantingly across the wide, empty fields outside my window on the north side of the house; I see the white road going towards town. . . .
>
> Dear Miss Guilford, do you remember the time we stole the cherry pies? . . . The pies were just from the oven—hot and fresh and tempting—and they had been incautiously placed on a window ledge (to cool), just within our reach! Nellie C.—(the boldest because the oldest of us), proposed it, and instantly we carried out her idea. When summoned before the Professor, how we trembled! But when he had us before him—with the door closed—he did nothing but laugh. . . . I am afraid I have forgotten most of my Latin—learned from you and from him; but it comes in play with Italian, which I now have to speak. . . .

From England in 1890 she wrote Miss Guilford:

> For myself, I feel that I owe you much. The pains you took with my crude compositions; the clearness with which you made my careless eyes notice the essential differences between a good style and a bad one; your praise, when I (not very often) deserved it; your discriminating, careful censure, which did me more good than all—these were, and still are, invaluable to me. I must have tried your patience, and I might, no doubt, have profited much more than I did, from your teachings. But it was the start you gave to the faint taste which enabled it later to grow in the right direction. (At least I hope it is right.)[10]

Miss Guilford remembered Connie Woolson as a "slender, blue-eyed maiden" ("at once fun-loving and dignified" and "always the center of a select, admiring group") whose hair lightly waved over her forehead and whose essays were "read in [a] low, cultured, voice" that held her schoolmates in "rapt attention." She was well liked by both her teachers and fellow pupils. A good student and avid reader, she also enjoyed taking long walks in the "Water Cure Woods" and rowing for miles on the Cuyahoga River, two means of exercise which she was always thereafter to delight in and to perform regularly.

In the summer of 1855, Constance made her first voyage to Mackinac Island, the Fairy Island of the Indians that lies in the straits between Lake Huron and Lake Michigan, and a place that was to mean much to her both in terms of personal pleasure and of literary capital. The family had a "summer cottage" at Mackinac, and the young girl grew to love the "charming" natural scenery of the island and to enjoy "the spicery of cedars and juniper alternating with the fresh forest-odors of young maples and beeches."[11] The freshness of the scene and the charm of the island's history appealed to Constance's sense of the picturesque; and later, when she began to consider literature as a career, two of her first contributions to the magazines were about Mackinac.[12] Thereafter it appears in some of her sketches and, chiefly, in *Anne* (1882), her first novel.

When, at the age of eighteen, Constance was graduated at the head of her class from Madame Chegaray's [13] "fashionable New York school," Mr. Woolson took the whole family as a special treat, according to Clara Woolson Benedict, Connie's younger sister, "on a long trip to all the places he and mother had lived in when they were young and happy, and before their awful losses fell upon them." "So," continues Mrs. Benedict, "Connie had a grand time."

> Father went to all the fashionable resorts around Boston, and Connie was a great belle. But the literary talent in her led her to do things that those *not* thus gifted, did not do. Mother often said to her: 'Connie, do not carry an inkstand up and down stairs as you do—you will some day fall and injure yourself, and spoil one of your pretty new dresses!'
>
> So one day the fall came, and I saw it! Connie was not injured; she had on a lovely grey costume, very becoming and beautifully made—she started to come down the steep hotel stairs, holding a

portfolio (she was planning to write on the piazza) and on the top of the limp portfolio stood her ink bottle with no cork in it! She stumbled and went down and the whole bottle of black ink poured over this lovely dress![14]

II *The Civil War*

The Civil War was not only the most important public event of Constance Woolson's life, but the excitement and the unusual character of the times apparently led her to think that she had fallen in love with a young officer in the army. Her reaction to the first days of the war itself is well expressed in *Anne*:

> April. The sound of military music; the sound of feet keeping step exactly, and overcoming by its regularity the noise of thousands of other feet hurrying on irregularly in front of them, abreast of them, and behind them. A crowd in the square so dense that that no one could pass through; the tree branches above black with boys; the windows all around the four sides filled with heads. And everywhere women pressing forward, waving handkerchiefs, some pallid, some flushed, but all deeply excited, forgetful of self, with eyes fixed on the small compact lines of military caps close together, moving steadily onward in the midst of the accompanying throng. And happy the one who had a place in the front rank: how she gazed! If a girl, no matter how light of heart and frivolous, a silence and soberness came over her for a moment, and her eyes grew wistful. If a woman, one who had loved, no matter how hard and cold she had grown, a warmer heart came back to her then, and tears rose [353-54].

Long after the war was over, she wrote her friend Edmund Clarence Stedman: ". . . the war was the heart and spirit of my life, and everything has seemed tame to me since. Many persons do not feel so—I find. But I feel so, and cannot help it. I cannot even now hear the old war-tunes, or pass those soldiers' cemeteries at the South, or see an old flag, without choking up and turning away my head."[15] Even as late as 1890, her memories of the war were still green, for she remarked in a letter to Miss Guilford from Cairo, Egypt:

> Eugene Schuyler gave a house-warming on Easter Monday. A lady present invited me to her room in the evening and I went. As I entered the parlor the piano was sounding forth the strains of 'Tenting on the Old Camp Ground.' A company, of whom Elihu

> Vedder the artist was one, were singing the chorus and from that we passed to 'Rally Round the Flag' and 'Marching Through Georgia.' It was very strange under the shadow of the Pyramids, as it were. I belong to the generations, you know, who felt those years [of the war] as they have felt nothing since.[16]

There is little information available concerning Miss Woolson's day-to-day activities during the war. That she did what she could to contribute to the war effort is plain from several comments she made after the war was over. In an article published by *Lippincott's Magazine* in May, 1871, she commented that "during the war I took charge of a post-office in one of our huge sanitary fairs, and among my literary wares I was so fortunate as to procure a number of autographs . . ." ("Spots," 543). Among these "literary wares," she wrote Stedman on July 8, 1877, was a letter from Hawthorne, "always" one of her "gods": "I have a letter from Hawthorne, written to me when I was postmistress at a Sanitary Fair in reply to one asking for autographs. I have it among my treasures. . . ."

Perhaps the most interesting matter to come to light recently in regard to Miss Woolson's life during the war is her brief encounter with romance. Few details are available, but in two unpublished letters written in January, 1891, and December, 1893, to Samuel Mather, she recalls her feelings for Colonel Zeph Spaulding of Cleveland, a childhood friend and former associate editor of a "little manuscript newspaper" she had produced at Mackinac one summer. "The glamor," she observed in the first of these letters, "that the war threw over the young officers who left their homes to fight, made me fancy I cared for him. But I see now that it was never a serious feeling." Her next mention of Spaulding occurred in one of the last letters she ever wrote: "I should like to see him again," she informed her nephew. "If I could get him *alone*, I dare say we should have a very friendly and funny talk. But, meanwhile, we should both be inwardly thinking, 'Great heavens—what an escape I had!' It was only the glamor of the war that brought us together. Every girl wanted to have a soldier-lover in those intense years, and every soldier (especially the volunteers) was wrought up to the highest point of excitement & romance."

Miss Woolson's romantic notions about soldiers and war probably did not outlast the war itself. In a revealing passage in

Anne, for example, she comments omnisciently on the illusions of a "volunteer assistant, a young girl," who is excited "over the opportunity afforded her to help and comfort 'our poor dear wounded heroes.' The wounded heroes," the author suggests wryly, "were not poetical in appearance; they were simply a row of ordinary sick men, bandaged in various ways, often irritable, sometimes profane; their grammar was defective, and they cared more for tobacco than for texts, or even poetical quotations. The young nurse would soon have her romance rudely dispelled" (368).

III *Death and Transition*

With the end of the war, Constance turned her attention to other things. A young lady in her mid-twenties who already considered herself a spinster, she gave some thought to literature as a career and contributed anonymous articles, so Arthur Stedman has written, to Episcopal periodicals in the years immediately prior to 1870.[17]

Charles Jarvis Woolson's death in 1869 was the crucial event in her life in this period. Early in July of that year Mr. Woolson became ill, and though his physician thought he was doing well enough in late July for Connie to leave for Mackinac, he died on August 6, less than ten days after her departure from Cleveland.[18] Loving and respecting her father as she did, she was deeply affected by his death while she was on a pleasure trip. Twenty years later she had not ceased regretting her absence at the time of his death. One infers this from many references but especially from a letter she wrote to Samuel Mather in 1890 regarding the recent death of his father:

> I am thankful for your sakes that you were all with him during the last hours. You are spared the eternal regret that comes, when it has been otherwise. There is something extremely solemn, I think, in the death of a father, or mother; the children are touched to the inmost heart, & it is a moment like no other; face to face we then stand—with the great mystery.

That she inherited from her father his love of books and literature and nature (to say nothing of his deafness and of his fortitude in the face of trials and tragedy) there can be little doubt, and one may readily appreciate Richardson's point that "the daughter-father relationship" is "more adequately realized in her fiction that that of the daughter-mother" (32).

The death of the father broke up the Woolson home in Cleveland and was, according to Richardson, "the determining factor" which turned Constance "into the path of literary work." Kern had earlier suggested that "financial considerations may have influenced her decision in this matter." Whatever the reason—and the two views are hardly incompatible—she began to contribute descriptive articles and travel sketches to the great literary magazines in 1870 and letters about "Gotham" to the *Daily Cleveland Herald* and its *Supplement* (a paper edited by George A. Benedict, the father-in-law of Clara Woolson Benedict) in the winter of 1870-71.[19]

During this period she left Cleveland for good. For a time in 1870 and for the first few months of 1871 she lived in New York City, but when her mother's health began to demand a warmer climate and when Clara's husband was killed in a railroad accident in 1871, Constance became her mother's companion. Frequently in company with Clara and her young daughter Clare, the two lived in New York State during the summer and in the South during the winter and early spring.[20]

IV *Sojourn in the South*

In the autumn of 1873 Mrs. Woolson, in company with her two daughters and granddaughter, left New York for St. Augustine, Florida, by way of Richmond, Charleston, Savannah, and Jacksonville. Describing her first trip south for some of her Northern relatives, Mrs. Woolson remarked on the sights seen in each of the Southern cities and noted that Connie and Clara "sallied forth" in Richmond and Charleston to buy newspapers and guidebooks. St. Augustine proved congenial to the tastes of the little group; and the old town, as Kern has pointed out, soon became Miss Woolson's "literary capital in the South." Regarding her impression of her new surroundings, she wrote her old friend Arabella Carter Washburn:

> . . . The life here is so fresh, so new, so full of certain wild freedom. I walk miles through the hummocks, where it looks as though no one had ever walked before, gathering wild flowers everywhere, or sitting down under the pine trees to rest in the shade. . . . Then on other days I take a row boat and go prowling

> down the inlet into all sorts of creeks that go no one knows where; I wind through dense forests where the trees meet overhead, and the long grey moss brushes my solitary boat as I pass. I go far up the Sebastian River as utterly alone as Robinson Crusoe. I meet alligators, porpoises, pelicans, cranes, and even deer, but not a human soul. Then again I often sail out with the numerous gentlemen who have nothing else to do; we go outside into the broad ocean and plunge along over the blue waves with the bluest sky in the world overhead. . . . You know the ocean is new to me and I am so fond of it already that I feel as if I never cared to go inland any more. The little town is almost too lazy to breathe. The people apparently have no curiosity in their organization and you might stand on your head in the middle of their little plaza all day, and they would hardly turn to look at you, much less take the trouble to ask 'why.' You go and come at your pleasure, nobody knows or cares how or with whom. This, to me, is charming.[21]

Here she met people from all "points of the compass": rich Northerners seeking a comfortable resort town; sick Northerners seeking respite and surcease from harsh winters; army officers and their wives at the little military post; church people (chiefly Presbyterians and Episcopalians); and the mixed population indigenous to the town itself.

Here in the spring of 1874 she also met Edmund Clarence Stedman, the well-known poet and critic, who was in St. Augustine for a rest. Stedman took long walks over the pine barrens and on the sea-wall with Constance Woolson and was impressed with her qualities: "Rarely have [I] met," he wrote home, "so gentle, earnest, and brilliant a woman."[22]

This meeting in St. Augustine was the beginning of a long literary friendship especially valuable to the rising young author from Cleveland. A few months after their first meeting, she wrote him to acknowledge his friendly help: "Nobody begins to do so much for me as you do. I have been really touched by it, and you seem to me the most generous person in the world. . . ." In 1875 she remembered with gratitude one of their first meetings: "I believe I have told you 'all about myself,' at some length. It is one of your delightful habits to show real interest in other people's work. I remember how steadily and yet how quietly you kept the conversation on my affairs and myself that day on the sea-wall, and that evening on the beach." Two years later she informed him (apparently in response to his question) that, in regard to literature, he was the "only adviser" she had had.[23]

The growing popularity of St. Augustine as a resort center soon led Constance Woolson to complain to Stedman that it was "too fashionable and too expensive" for her tastes though she continued to go there with her mother until 1878. Actually her attachment to the little town (her "peculiar affection" for it, as Henry James later put it) and her fondness for Florida in general were both strongly marked. She had been in Europe only a month, for instance, when she wrote Stedman on December 28, 1877: ". . . I hardly appreciated myself, until I was separated from it, how much I loved that warm hazy peninsula where I spent five long happy winters with my dear Mother." Over and over again in her letters of the 1880's and 1890's she mentions that she plans to return to America and to make Florida her home.[24] On February 24, 1887, she wrote Stedman from Florence that she was planning to come home to live in Florida: "I am only waiting to store up a little more money; then I shall return; buy a wee cottage down there; set up a crane and three orange-trees; & never stir again." And after she had lived in many of Europe's finest resorts, she remarked to Samuel Mather in 1891 that Florida was "the best winter resort in the world."

In the pattern established by the Woolsons in the early 1870's, of living much of each year in Florida, they also spent some time in the mountains of Virginia, Tennessee, or North Carolina and frequently stayed a few weeks in Charleston. Constance was especially fond of the mountains of western North Carolina ("the scenery," she once wrote, "is far finer than any I have ever seen"), and she and her mother found time on several occasions to visit Asheville, then a little mountain village with few pretensions to being the resort center that her character Horace Chase later predicted it would become.

Miss Woolson enjoyed the "beloved N. C. mountains" and found native reading habits rather quaint. "Would you believe it," she observed in a letter to Stedman in 1874, "the people here have never even seen one of George Eliot's novels—have never so much as heard the names of Bret Harte or Joaquin Miller—and speak of Addison as one of the 'modern writers!' . . . And you must not suppose either that these people are without culture; far from it. Many of them are from old Charleston families, honored southern names. . . ." Her visits to Asheville bore fruit in "Up in the Blue Ridge," a long sketch that she collected in *Rodman the Keeper* (1880) and in *Horace Chase* (1894), her last novel, to say nothing of a descriptive article on "The French Broad" published by *Harper's* in April, 1875. The scene in *For the Major* (1883), her only novelette, is set in this same general area. Thus it was that she gathered background and local-color materials for use in her fiction.

Charleston she found a fascinating city. She liked its homes and its culture, and she admired the aristocratic ladies and gentlemen of the old families who had lost all in the war. The city, she once remarked, "has a character of its own, and is like nothing but itself." Much of her interest in the history of the city and in its landmarks and great estates is expressed in "Up the Ashley and Cooper," a long lead article published by *Harper's* in December, 1875. She described her emotions regarding this piece in a letter written in the fall of 1875 to Paul Hamilton Hayne, a well-known contemporary Southern poet and a native of Charleston: ". . . I wrote it with the pleasantest feelings of interest in the subject, and treated it with much more care and courtesy than I should have done had I been writing of the Vicinity of Boston."[25] Earlier in the same year she had described the place and her reactions to it in a letter of April 25 to Samuel Mather:

> It is charming here—the most picturesque city I have ever seen. . . . I went to the top of St. Michael's the other evening to see the city and the bay by moonlight; for some unexplained reason the historic harbor was much more distinct than it ever is by daylight, every outline of Sumter clearly visible, Moultrie standing out on the north point of the mainland . . . , and, opposite, the long low spit of Cumming Point, Morris Island, where the remains of Battery Wagner could be distinguished. Turning the other way there lay the city between its two rivers, silvery ribbons in the moonlight, shining with lights from side to side. Battered, ruined, poverty-stricken as it is, it impresses me as the most aristocratic city I have ever seen. The old houses with their great walls and shut-in gardens are prouder now even in ruin than anything we can show at the north. You see they had kept up the old manorial —almost feudal—ideas and customs, living with their slaves around them. Of course such things are as effete as moated castles now-a-days; but they are picturesque.

On July 23 she wrote Hayne that she had "never understood" the pride of South Carolinians until she had come "down among you." "Why," she continued, "you seem to me the proudest people on the face of the globe! The blue blooded Castillians can be nothing to you. There is a height, and a breadth, and a depth, to your pride, which actually goes beyond even the comprehension of a plain Yankee woman like myself.—And (another thing I did not understand until I came down south myself) there *is* cause and reason for your pride. You *do* bear the marks of your old Cavalier descent, and, in spite of my unwillingness, I am forced to acknowledge it. I have never seen such courtly manners as those of the elderly Charlestonians; I mean rather, those whose manners were formed in ante bellum days."[26] Three years later, in August, 1878, she published anonymously in the Contributors' Club of the *Atlantic Monthly* a charming essay in which she described approvingly the old-fashioned manners of the South Carolina gentlemen she had mentioned to Hayne and the old-fashioned reading tastes of Charlestonians she had discussed in other letters of this period.

On the whole, she liked the South and sympathized with its plight during the years of Reconstruction. She was aware of its shortcomings—"the yellow fever," "the insolence of the blacks," and "the bitterness of the whites." After long periods of residence there, she was glad to return to the North, as she wrote Stedman on July 23, 1876: "Think of three long years among people who say 'gee-arden' and 'street-ce-arr,' who talk about Addison and the 'Spectator,' and who mix up 'Christian Reid' [a minor North Carolina novelist of the period] and her feeble stories with the great English Charles of the same name! I like the Southerners; but it depresses one to live too long among them." Two months earlier, on May 14, she had written Hayne on the same theme: "I like the South; no Yankee-born Northerner ever liked it better; but, three years away from home! . . . The spirit of this letter has its face turned northward, as you see. You must excuse it."[27]

Nevertheless she planned to return to St. Augustine in November, for the climate and the picturesqueness of the South appealed to her despite her strong opinions concerning slavery and the recent war.[28] She was scarcely in Europe a month before she was writing back about her love for Florida and her plans to return there some day; and when she came to write a preface for *Rodman the Keeper*: *Southern Sketches* (1880), she could only refer to the impossibility of recording "the inward charm of that beautiful land which the writer has learned to love, and from which she now severs herself with true regret."

During her sojourn in the South, *Castle Nowhere*: *Lake-Country Sketches* (1875), her first book of fiction written for adults, appeared. At the same time she was hard at work exploiting the new Southern materials in her stories and sketches, and within a few months after her departure from the South, *Rodman the Keeper*, a collection of her best tales with Southern backgrounds, was published in New York.

Mrs. Woolson, in the meantime, had died in Florida on February 13, 1879, in her seventieth year; and Constance, then almost thirty-nine, was free to live her own life, though it took her some time to recover from her mother's death. In March she described the pain and sorrow to Stedman: "I am so desolate without my Mother that I cannot speak of it. The whole world is changed to me. . . . I have got to learn how to live, over again." And, in a letter presumably written in the summer of 1880, she reminisced with her old friend Jane Averell Carter about Mrs. Carter's understanding and sympathy at the time of Mrs. Woolson's death: "But you *did* say something of worth to me when I was suffering . . . I have not forgotten it; you wrote that you believed that, by my care, I had prolonged Mother's life for years. No one else has said this to me; I had not thought of it in that way myself. But it comforted me more than once, when I was tormented by the thought that if I had only done this, or that—perhaps I might have saved her . . ." (Benedict, II, 24-25).

V *The Pilgrim Abroad*

When she had recovered from the first intense grief over her mother's death, Constance Woolson, confronting the problem of reorienting her private life and having recently finished her first novel, decided to go to Europe to live for a while. She had always wanted to go there, as one readily recalls from her remarks in her youthful letter to Flora Payne. On June 15, 1875, she had confided to Hayne: "For I am outward bound; for the old world, before *very* long, I hope." In company with Clara Woolson Benedict and little Clare Benedict, she sailed from New York on the steamship *Gallia* in the middle of November and arrived in

England at the end of the month to begin a sojourn in the Old Country that was to last (though she did not know it at the time) for the rest of her life.[29]

After visiting in England for several weeks and recording in a letter of December 8, 1879, to Samuel Mather her impressions based upon some serious sight-seeing in London with Baedeker in hand, and upon such less serious "entertainments" as an "English Punch and Judy" enjoyed by both aunt and niece, Miss Woolson and company departed for France. She found Paris "fairly blockaded with ice and snow" and the whole country in the midst of "the coldest season in the present *century*!" Fleeing from the severe winter (she detested cold weather: "let the air grow really cold," she once remarked, "and down I go towards the gates of death"), the little party hurried southward to Mentone on the French Riviera. There the warm air revived them, and Miss Woolson, "perfectly charmed," took notes that later appeared in a two-part descriptive article in *Harper's*.[30]

After a pleasant stay of almost three months on the "sunny shore" of Mentone, where Constance worked hard on the manuscript of *For the Major*, the sisters proceeded to Florence by way of Genoa and Pisa. From the city of Dante and Giotto she wrote Samuel Mather on March 20, 1880, explaining an important principle of her approach to seeing Europe: ". . . the only way I can manage 'Europe,' and my own life here, is to settle down for a number of months in each place. . . . So I shall see Europe slowly, and by no means extensively; but I shall see and enjoy thoroughly the places I *do* see . . ." (Benedict, II, 181). Thus she decided to stay in Florence, a city that "enchanted" her, for several months and, later, to make it a sort of winter headquarters for much of each year. On her first visit she and Mrs. Benedict stayed at a "well-known 'pension' " in one of the "old palaces of the Medici," and she gave her usual serious attention to the history and art of the places she visited. She looked at the pictures in the Pitti Palace "very slowly" and "let them 'grow' into her memory," and she studied "Florentine history" and books on art zealously and joyously. "Florence," she wrote a friend about this time, "is all that I have dreamed and more," and she continued:

> . . . here I have attained that old-world feeling I used to dream about, a sort of enthusiasm made up of history, mythology, old churches, pictures, statues, vineyards, the Italian sky, dark-eyed

> peasants, opera-music, Raphael and Old Michael, 'Childe Harold,' the 'Marble Faun,' 'Romola,' and ever so many more ingredients—the whole having, I think, taken me pretty well off my feet! Perhaps I ought to add Henry James. He has been perfectly charming to me for the last three weeks. . . [Benedict, II, 184-85].

Henry James, or at least his work, was no stranger to Constance Woolson. In the 1870's she had read and liked some of his short stories; noted his "Florentine opinions" in *Transatlantic Sketches* (1875); had been "very much disappointed" in *Roderick Hudson* (1876); and had praised *The Europeans* (1878) in two anonymous critical essays in the *Atlantic* in 1879. Upon arriving in London in December of that year, she had looked up James only to discover that he was in Paris; but he made up for his absence in the winter by becoming, in Florence next spring, something of a gallant and knowledgeable cicerone to a fellow artist whose feeling for the Old World and whose enthusiasm for its culture must have reminded him more than once of his own Cornelia Spencer in "Four Meetings" (1877). Miss Woolson has described James's attentions in a letter written at this time: "He was very kind to me. He has many acquaintances in Florence and he was constantly invited out to lunch and dinner parties; yet with all this, he found time to come in the mornings and take me out; sometimes to the galleries or churches, and sometimes just for a walk in the beautiful green Cascine. . . . His criticisms were new and remarkable, at least to me. I mean that he chose such remarkable things to admire!" (Benedict, II, 185n).

James was especially helpful in the matter of tutoring his friend in her study of Florentine art ("he knows," she commented in a letter, "the pictures as well as I know Florida," but, as always, she maintained her integrity and decided to be "perfectly honest" and not admire what she actually "did *not* admire"). James's interest in Constance Woolson was, as Kern has pointed out, "not confined to the guidance of her study of art." "Both of these writers," Kern goes on to say, "were interested in depicting the effects of the continental environment on Americans" (116). One may also suggest that these two mature people felt for each other an immediate affinity that was the natural consequence of similar tastes, opinions, and intellectual interests and of a corresponding quest on the part of each in a fascinating, romantic old world.[31]

At the urging of her sister, Miss Woolson unwillingly left Florence and traveled northward to Venice in June. There, in the "Water City," as she sometimes calls it, she found another kind of enchantment; and for a week that she was sure would "remain like a lovely dream" in her mind forever, she was charmed by the sights (the Piazza and domes of San Marco, and Doges' Palace, the Bridge of Sighs); the "sumptuous" Venetian pictures (particularly Titian's "Assumption" and "Presentation in the Temple" and the Bellini Madonnas); the Grand Canal and the gondolas ("I shall always say the perfection of earthly motion is a gondola"); and "the music of bands of singers with guitars." She summed up her reaction to Venice in a letter of June 8 to her nephew: "After having heard of it and dreamed of it and looked at pictures of it all my life, I find the reality even more picturesque and wonderful than my expectations. This, I think, is quite remarkable. Remember how many long years I have been imagining!" (Benedict, II, 216-17).

From Venice the travelers went to Milan, where they spent a day or two looking at the "beautiful cathedral" and Leonardo's "Last Supper," which made a "great impression" on them. Then they went to Como, to Lugano, and through the St. Gotthard Pass into Switzerland and to Lake Lucerne, where they stopped at Beckenried, "a very quiet, small rural village on the south shore of the lake, about an hour by boat from Lucerne" (Benedict, II, 221).

This progression from Florence to Switzerland became something of a pattern which Miss Woolson (and occasionally her sister and niece) followed each year. The autumns and winters were spent in Florence (with occasional visits to Rome, "the most magical place in the world") and the summers in Switzerland or in the Black Forest of Germany. Often in the spring she went to Venice and stayed until the early part of the summer. In the autumn of 1883 she went to England for an extended stay and lived chiefly in London and Warwickshire until the spring of 1886, when she returned to Florence. There she occupied first the Villa Castellani, at Bellosguardo, a large estate described as the Villa Dorio in "Dorothy," and after January 1, 1887, she leased the Villa Brichieri in the same neighborhood. In her nine-room apartment with its "unrivalled" view commanding "not only the 'sweet Val d'Arno' . . . but all Florence with its domes and towers," she was at last able to make a semi-permanent home for herself.[32] She lived in the Villa Brichieri for almost three years, leaving finally in the late months of 1889 to make the trip to the Greek Islands and to Athens that she described in an article for *Harper's* in August, 1892. From Athens she presumably sailed for Cairo by way of Crete, and in the early months of 1890 she fell prey to the fascination of Egypt. On February 19 she wrote Professor Willard Fiske, her American friend and neighbor in Florence: "We [Mrs. Benedict and Clare were with her] spent a month in Cairo. I am so fascinated with the place that I am thinking of staying there through March, and perhaps part of April, alone. I could not give a stronger proof of my liking. . . ."[33] Her experiences in Egypt provided her with material for a long two-part essay that appeared in *Harper's* in the October and November issues of 1891 (Benedict, II, 344n).

On her return from Egypt, Miss Woolson went to England and began her last novel, *Horace Chase* (1894), in the late spring of 1890 at Cheltenham in Gloucestershire, where she enjoyed taking long walks, seeing the old churches and abbeys, and rowing on "Shakespeare's Avon." In August, 1891, she went to Oxford for a stay of more than two years. She was "perfectly captivated" by the university town:

> Oh, it is *so* lovely here! The grey quadrangles of the twenty-one colleges, all so beautiful and so different; the lovely college gardens; the two rivers and little row-boats; the beautiful country all about . . . I have endless pleasure before me. . . .
>
> I am perfectly captivated with Oxford. I have had some lovely afternoons on the two little rivers; far up the Cherwell under the trees—it is enchanting. Then the old gardens of the colleges are ideal. And all the beautiful towers, facades, gateways, chapels, etc., etc. [Benedict, II, 369-70].

She made good use of her time in Oxford. She worked very hard on her new novel, and for relaxation she took long walks in the country or rowed on the little rivers or, on occasion, journeyed to London for some special event such as the first-night performance of Henry James's *The American* in October, 1891. James in turn visited her in Oxford, and they talked about writing a play together. Otherwise, she was amused by the "gaieties of 'Boat Week'," and she enjoyed walking across the beautiful Oxford countryside where some of the landmarks reminded her of "Thyrsis" and "The Scholar Gipsy," two of her favorite poems by Matthew Arnold. In the late fall of 1892 she took a trip down the Thames "in a small steamer, to see the scenery" and "made a little pilgrimage to Stoke-Poges where Gray is buried." In the same year she wrote Mrs. Samuel Mather to describe her life in Oxford and to sum up her response to it: "I think you were right in saying that you felt convinced that Oxford would be more satisfactory to me than any place outside of Italy. It is" (Benedict, II, 374). Her last experience in England, however, was an unpleasant one. In the early summer of 1893 she left Oxford to return to Italy. On her way she stopped in London to see a dentist and contracted "a sharp attack of influenza," her "first experience"—but, alas, not her last—with this "malady."

After her bout with the flu, she went on to Venice and found it "more beautiful, more enchanting than ever." There she wrote her niece, Katharine Livingston Mather, on July 2, 1893: "I haven't got back my strength, and I have always heard that weakness and depressed spirits were the special charms of this delightful complaint" (Benedict, II, 379). This remark, as Kern has suggested, may provide a clue to the mystery surrounding Miss Woolson's death in the following January. Her weakness, however, did not prevent her from pursuing a rather rigorous daily schedule and from taking on the responsibilities of renting two floors of a "furnished house" for eight months (beginning September 10, 1893). She described her daily routine in a letter of August 20 to Miss Mather:

> I am now called at 4:30 every morning, and then, after a cup of tea, I sit (in a dressing-gown) and write until 9:30, when I have breakfast. This is to get the cool hours for work. Then I dress and go on writing until 4 p. m., when I go to the Lido and take a sea-bath. These baths are, to me, quite perfect; the best I have ever had, because not at all cold. . . . Then home to dinner at 7:30, and all the evening I am out in my gondola. . . . Nothing in the world can be more beautiful than the lagoons in the evening [Benedict, II, 380].

At this time she was working on the galley proofs of *Horace Chase,* her last serialized novel for *Harper's.* After she finished these, she apparently took a rest from writing for a few months, though she planned to "begin a new novel on January 1st."

VI *Death in Venice*

In these last months of her life, in spite of her love for Venice, her pleasure in her new apartment, and her general satisfaction with Venetian life (especially the climate and the society, which she preferred to that of Florence), her old enemy—melancholia—settled in for a siege. Years earlier, on July 23, 1876, she had written Stedman about these fits of depression: ". . . I am overweighted with a sort of depression that comes unexpectedly, and makes everything black. My grandfather gave up to it and was a dreary useless man; my father battled against it all his life, and again and again warned me about it; but I was young then, and only half believed in it. Now, he is gone, and it has come to me. I try to conquer it and sometimes I succeed, sometimes I—don't." And in an undated letter—probably written while she was in Europe—to Mrs. Washburn, Miss Woolson observes to her old friend: "Don't fancy I am sad all the time. Oh no. I am much too busy and full of plans of all kinds. But at times, in spite of all I can do, this deadly enemy of mine creeps in, and once in, he is master. I think it is constitutional, and I know it is inherited" (Benedict, I, 244n).

Constance Woolson, however, was not basically pessimistic about life. As a good Episcopalian, she held that this life, though difficult at times, had much to offer, a view she expressed in a letter of September 10, 1876, to Paul Hayne: "I think we may safely trust our Creator as to the next life. Neither, have I ever been able to see the black side of this [life]. I think it is a very beautiful and generally speaking a very good sort of world; all we want is a little improvement in man."

Nevertheless, by December, 1893, the "deadly enemy" had taken hold; in two separate letters, references to its presence are clear. The first of these was written to Katharine Mather on Christmas Eve: "I am invited to-night to a Christmas party at Lady Layard's. . . . I have declined, and shall sit alone by my fire and read Dickens' Christmas Carol and Milton's Hymn on the Nativity and think of those who are gone" (Benedict, II, 391). In much the same vein Miss Woolson wrote Mrs. Washburn on the same day:

> I am invited to-night to a beautiful Christmas party at Lady Layard's, but I prefer to sit alone by my fire and think of

days that are gone. . . . I often think that though I stay abroad, I seem to remember better than any one else. All the others have forgotten the old personages, but I haven't. . . . I have taught myself to be calm and philosophic, and I feel perfectly sure that the next existence will make clear all the mysteries and riddles of this. In the meantime, one can do one's duty or try to do it. But . . . if at any time you should hear that I have gone, I want you to know beforehand that my end was peace, and even joy at release . . . [Benedict, II, 392-93].

With the exception of a business letter to Harper and Brothers dated January 19, 1894, this letter to Mrs. Washburn is the last personal communication of which there is any accurate record.[34]

In January Miss Woolson contracted influenza for the second time within a period of seven months, and this dread malady gave way to typhoid fever, according to Dr. W. W. Baldwin, her friend and physician. On January 24, 1894, she either fell or threw herself from her bedroom window while her nurse was momentarily out of the room. Shortly thereafter she was picked up from the street below by her own gondolier and brought back to her apartment where she died before daybreak without having regained consciousness.

The circumstances surrounding Miss Woolson's death are, as Kern has pointed out, "controversial and impossible to determine with finality," and there is no new evidence to adduce today. Kern's decision to give the facts and "allow the reader to draw his own conclusions" is still a reasonable one. Before proper conclusions may be drawn, however, one should keep in mind several things about Constance Woolson. She was a faithful Christian and therefore theoretically opposed to suicide, regardless of the circumstances (as Margaret Harold says in *East Angels*: "'I am so wretched . . . that only my firm belief that my Creator knows best has enabled me to live on, has kept me from ending it'"). In this regard one may remember her letter to Hayne quoted above. She firmly believed that her Creator knew best. In the second place, despite the depression clearly evident in her letters to Miss Mather and Mrs. Washburn, she had made plans to write a new novel and to live in Venice for some months (in a letter of December 13 she says "some years") before returning to Florida to retire. Moreover, she usually felt depressed after finishing a book. Earlier in 1893 she had written Samuel Mather that she was "pretty low in health" but no worse than she had been "at the end" of her "two preceding books"; and she still had "two parts more" of *Horace Chase* to complete when this was written. Finally, with regard to her death itself, it seems reasonably clear (of course there is no conclusive proof) that she was delirious near the end. Either influenza or typhoid fever could have induced this delirium in Miss Woolson's case, for she had been a victim of throat trouble for years and had on occasion been delirious as a result of one respiratory ailment or another.[35]

On January 31, 1894, the body of Constance Fenimore Woolson was buried in the Protestant Cemetery in Rome, the last resting place also of Keats and Shelley. The details of the funeral were handled by Mrs. Grace Carter, a relative and devoted friend, and by John Hay, the writer and diplomat who was an old friend and Samuel Mather's brother-in-law. Mrs. Benedict and Clare were in the United States at the time, though they made arrangements to sail for Europe in March in order to take care of Miss Woolson's personal effects and to pack the furnishings of her apartment in Venice. When they visited the cemetery in Rome before going to Venice, Mrs. Benedict made her decision concerning the proper memorial for the grave:

> After seeing the cemetery, the stone that I had thought of putting there seemed entirely out of place—the slope of the land making a high cross not suitable; so . . . finding the plot filled with growing violets (already arranged by Colonel and Mrs. John Hay), I decided to place a wide, handsome marble coping all around the flower bed, with simply 'Constance Fenimore Woolson, 1894,' upon it and to have a Celtic cross of white marble laid flat down on the bed of violets, as the Roman climate is mild enough to make the certainty of violets living all the year round. Ivy is to be planted at the base of the coping [Benedict, III, 3].

Henry James, who had spent "many weeks" in Venice helping the Benedicts to clear Constance Woolson's apartment, was much impressed by the grave. Years later, in 1907, he wrote Clare: ". . . the most beautiful thing in Italy, almost, seemed to me in May and June last, the exquisite summery luxuriance and perfect tendance of that spot. I mean, of course, that very particular spot below the great grey wall, the cypresses and the timesilvered Pyramid. It is tremendously, inexhaustibly touching—its effect never fails to overwhelm" (Benedict, III, 266). In the light of such a statement, one cannot help being reminded of John Marcher's visit to the grave of May Bartram in "The Beast in the Jungle" (1903).

VII A "*Remarkable and Unforgettable Personality*"

In such brief compass one can do little more than suggest Constance Woolson's personal character, but, fortunately, Clare Benedict has commented perspicaciously on her aunt's "remarkable and unforgettable personality." Constance Woolson "never failed to win a person if she desired to do so," Miss Benedict has remarked, "for her charm was potent and well-nigh irresistible." She had a "passionate and even stormy temperament, together with a keenly analytical mind. But she was capable, so her niece has averred, of "such intense sympathy with and understanding of all forms of suffering, whether physical or mental, as well as all moral and intellectual aspirations, that she was able to draw out of people the best that was in them, while giving in return the most inspiring and comforting comprehension." She was also a "delightful talker" and an "excellent listener" and her "humor was kindly." On occasion "she suffered from periodical fits of acute depression, but her powers of enjoyment were correspondingly high, and her interests were many and catholic."

She loved the out-of-doors, wild flowers, ferns, walking, boating, rowing, dogs, and plays. Her love for music was especially great, but after the mid-1870's an "increasing deafness" obliged her "to turn to pictures for some measure of that mental delight and stimulus which she had formerly derived from music." And, Miss Benedict has added justly, "her courageous determination in so doing was but another proof of her strong character." She was an avid reader all her life, and she enjoyed "society" under certain conditions which she usually observed.[36] Her personal appearance, which she deprecated, must have been attractive, for she had a "fine carriage and poise of the head, beautiful hands, and a delicate, almost transparent complexion," and "there was about her," as Miss Benedict has observed, "an air of distinction which no likeness has fully reproduced."[37]

She was, then, a handsome woman and one of great talent. The qualities of her mind and character have been "epitomize[d] in a wonderful way," as Miss Benedict has pointed out, in a "Reflection," a passage in her notebook written on Christmas Eve, 1893: "I should like to turn into a peak when I die; to be a beautiful purple mountain, which would please the tired, sad eyes of thousands of human beings for ages. For 'I will lift up mine eyes unto the hills, from whence cometh my help,' is an almost universal aspiration" (Benedict, II, 411). To the jaded sensibilities of many readers in the twentieth century, Constance Fenimore Woolson's life and work may well offer the aid to the human spirit she contemplated in this meditation.

CHAPTER 2

The "Immeasurable World of Print": The Short Fiction

CONSTANCE WOOLSON'S first contributions to the great national magazines were descriptive articles in the guise of fiction. She wrote of the Zoar Community in the Tuscarawas Valley of Ohio, of Mackinac in the far north of the Lake country, and of Lake Otsego near the ancestral home of the Coopers. Gradually she began to concentrate more on her characters and less on description, though she never lost her concern for setting and background even after she had lived for years in Europe. Her first sketches and stories dealt, with few exceptions, with the country she knew best—the Great Lakes area, Ohio, and New York. Later, after she had lived for some time in the South, she began to treat Southern characters and scenes in her fiction. Finally, when she had spent many years in Europe, she began to use European (especially Italian) characters and settings in her tales, though her favorite approach at this point in her career was to place Americans in Old World backgrounds. Thus she took advantage of her experience and of her knowledge of place to produce more than enough fiction to comprise four volumes of short stories: *Castle Nowhere* (1875); *Rodman the Keeper* (1880); *The Front Yard* (1895); and *Dorothy* (1896).

I *Castle Nowhere*

Though she had won a prize for a volume she had written for children in 1872, Miss Woolson considered *Castle Nowhere: Lake-Country Sketches* her first book.[1] In it she brought together nine stories, all of which (with the exception of the title piece which was appearing for the first time) had been published first in the pages of the *Atlantic Monthly, Scribner's Monthly, Harper's New Monthly*, the *Galaxy*, and *Appletons' Journal*. These pieces, selected from a number of sketches dealing with lake-country settings and characters, represent, on the whole, her best work in this vein, though there are several other stories that might have been included in this volume.[2]

James R. Osgood, the Boston publisher, apparently suggested to Miss Woolson in 1874 that he would be interested in bringing out a collection of her best sketches. After an agreement was reached, the volume was scheduled for publication in 1875. On January 20 of that year she wrote Stedman about her forthcoming book: "I do not know whether you will approve of my volume, or rather, of any volume at all from me at present. But it seemed to me best to make a beginning, and it is a modest one, the best of my stories led by one which gives the name to the collection. Please keep this secret at present, as I have told no one. . . . The whole collection belongs to the lake-country."

The book appeared a month or two later and was, on the whole, favorably received by the critics. A reviewer in *Appletons' Journal*, April 3, 1875, thought, for example, that the "promise" of this early work presaged a "very bright" literary future and that Miss Woolson had made "a contribution of something fresh and vigorous beyond the common" (439). Howells' criticism in the June *Atlantic* found much to praise in many of the stories —especially those which had first appeared in the *Atlantic's* own pages—and in the author's concern for "truth to human nature," though the champion of realism was "harassed . . . by a disagreeable fantasticality" in "Castle Nowhere."

That sketch, by the way, had been written especially for this collection and had therefore not appeared first in a magazine. If one needed to advance other reasons for the story's failure to come out in one of the great monthlies, they are ready at hand. It is, for example, very long (it runs to ninety-one pages in book form), and the central character espouses principles repugnant to the family reading circles so important to magazine circulation in the late nineteenth century. Furthermore, the story centers around a love that supersedes moral principles, but this is no ordinary love story, for the love described is that of a foster father for the child he has reared.

In order to get away from the trappings of civilization, Jarvis Waring goes into the wilderness "bordering the head of Lake

Michigan." There he chances to meet an old man named Amos Fog, who steals certain of Waring's possessions. In his search for the thief, Waring discovers a beautiful girl named Silver living in a log fortress called Castle Nowhere. (At this point readers of Cooper are likely to recall the "castle" in *The Deerslayer.*) Waring locates his stolen treasures and remains to find that Silver considers Fog her father and to be told Fog's story: he is an escaped murderer performing expiation through his loving concern for the girl—"a life for a life." Fog will do anything for Silver. He lures lake steamers to their doom in order to provide for her needs, telling himself that the crews lost are nothing to Silver's "delicate life." Yet he refuses to let her know the Bible, for "religion is fancy."

Before Waring becomes completely enthralled by Silver's naïveté, he leaves the castle, but is later rescued by Fog from the ice and cold. Finally surrendering to his feelings for the girl, Waring agrees to marry her, but he insists that they return to civilization after the ceremony. After leaving, however, Silver persuades him to return to Castle Nowhere, where they find Fog dying. They watch over the old man in his last hours, and he tells them he is "content," though his last words—"Is it expiated, O God?"—receive "no answer . . . on earth." With the death of Fog, the lovers leave the castle to fall in ruin and to become "indeed Nowhere."

Fog's lack of regard for conventional religion and his adoption of any means to a good end (i.e., the comfort and protection of Silver) did not endear him as a character to Miss Woolson's readers, a number of whom wrote to her questioning this aspect of his make-up. In an undated letter presumably written in 1875, Miss Woolson took up this matter with her friend Mrs. Washburn:

> At least twenty awful letters have I received because I made 'Old Fog' say he did not believe in eternal punishment. Is it possible that I am to be held personally responsible for the theology and morality of all my characters? I want you to think of me not as your old friend, when you read my writings, but as a 'writer,' like anyone else. For instance, take 'Adam Bede.' . . . Would you like to have a friend of yours the author of such a story? Dealing with such subjects? And yet it was a great book. . . . The truth is, Belle, whatever one does must be done with one's might and I would rather be strong than beautiful, or even good, provided the 'good' must be dull. All this applies

> more to what I hope to do in the future, of course, than to the slight sketches I have already brought out [Benedict, II, 20].

Even the critics were concerned. Howells' review in the *Atlantic* put it this way:

> A subtle confusion of all the conceptions of right and wrong is wrought by this old reprobate's devotion to the child, and his inability to feel that any means to her pleasure and comfort can be bad; but we doubt whether this is an intended effect, and if it is, we think it not worth the writer's or reader's pains. Castle Nowhere is the least satisfactory of the stories. . . [XXXV, 736].[3]

This aspect of Fog's character is hardly likely to disturb the modern reader. It is Fog's eagerness to sacrifice himself for the girl that may now arouse the wonder of readers, though it should be added that Fog's actions have been provided for in the motivation and analysis of his character. In this sense, Fog takes his place in a long line of Woolson characters who devote themselves to some unselfish goal. Fog is not altogether credible as a character, but neither is he completely "fantastical." The sketch's chief failure lies not so much in his confusion of right and wrong as it does in the failure of Waring and Silver to come off as believable human beings and in the introduction, as Kern has pointed out, of an "improbable series of events" into the narrative. Waring's conventional cynicism and Silver's wraithlike quality make the old outcast's elements of humanity appear all the more realistic by contrast. In the end, the sketch, though it is something less than an unqualified artistic success, is saved from total failure by the portrait of Fog and the vivid realization of the lake-country setting.

The next two pieces, "Peter the Parson" and "Jeannette," both appeared first in *Scribner's Monthly*.[4] "Peter the Parson" capitalizes, as the title implies, on the author's interest in Episcopal clergymen and is a study in dramatic contrast. The Reverend Herman W. Peters, a high-church Anglican priest, has come to a raw little settlement on Lake Superior as a missionary of his church; but he finds himself ridiculed by the Harte-like miners who inhabit the place and whose interest in religion can only be aroused by Brother Saul, a miner himself who enjoys "a-holding forth" among his comrades. The contrast between the two men themselves and the two widely divergent approaches to the faith they represent, to say nothing of the implied contrast between frontier and civilization, makes for a story rich in suggestion and overtone. Seldom in her tales did Miss Woolson elaborate anything more carefully fashioned than the poignant but never sentimental contrast she drew between the brawling, lusty settlement and the little, ascetic Anglican priest who, though he failed to convert the miners to his faith, lived up to it and died for it himself.[5]

Contrast is also vital in "Jeannette," in which a French half-breed girl is the central character. Her beauty and coquetry attract the attention of Rodney Prescott, the scion of an old New England family and an officer in the army at Mackinac Island, Miss Woolson's favorite summer resort and a natural background for much of her early fiction.[6] The contrast between Jeannette's ignorance and natural grace and Prescott's culture and acquired polish is skillfully developed in this sketch, and her scornful rejection of his suit in favor of one of her own kind is brought off nicely.

"The Old Agency," although it was published in the *Galaxy*, appeared in December, 1874, the same month as "Jeannette," and is a sort of companion piece to that tale. The setting and background of "The Old Agency" is Mackinac Island, and the narrator in both stories is Mrs. Sarah Corlyne, the aunt of an army officer at Fort Mackinac. In this work, however, the point of view is that of Father Piret, a beloved Roman Catholic priest whose aristocratic bearing and mysterious past have cast a romantic aura about a personality that is mythic in nature and substance. Piret's tale is about Jacques, an old and penniless soldier of the French Empire who has sought a place of refuge where he may dream of the glories of the past and prepare to die. The use of the double point of view in this instance provides less contrast than one might imagine, since Mrs. Corlyne is entirely sympathetic to Father Piret's qualities and to the loyalties of Jacques. If this point of contrast is not realized, the effort of the gentle old priest to infuse Christian precepts and attitudes into the grenadier's pagan worship of Napoleon affords Miss Woolson an opportunity subtly to contrast the two men as aliens and brothers and to show their different religions as expressive of two approaches to faith that are universal and timeless and that transcend the immediacy of the nineteenth century and Mackinac Island.

"Misery Landing," published in *Harper's* in May, 1874, is the only sketch in this collection to appear first in the monthly organ of the publishing firm with which Miss Woolson later made such pleasant arrangements concerning the publication of her work. Though its setting is an island near the western end of Lake Superior, its central character, John Jay, is from the metropolitan centers of sophistication and, in many ways, resembles Jarvis Waring in his cynical attitude. The contrast is strong between civilization and frontier, but the story does not quite come off because Jay fails to come alive, though his efforts to help others suggest some quality of humanity. The piece is chiefly interesting because of Jay's remarks regarding Bret Harte. In an entry in his diary, for example, he discusses Harte's "deep-hearted prose." "After all," he writes, "as long as I can read his pages, I can not be so bad as I seem, since, to my idea, there is more of goodness and generosity and courage in his words than in many a sermon. He shows us the good in the heart of the outcast." Later, he observes:

> I read aloud last evening. George [an ignorant boy of the region whom Jay has befriended] did not seem much interested in Bret Harte, but was captivated with the pageantry of 'Ivanhoe.' Strange that it should be so, but everywhere it is the cultivated people only who are taken with Bret. But they must be imaginative as well as cultivated; routine people, whether in life or in literature, dislike any thing unconventional or new [219].

Remembering her letter to Mrs. Washburn and not taking these views expressed by Jay as being too literally hers, one might yet suspect from reading this and other passages indicating similar opinions that Miss Woolson herself accepted the general tenor of these remarks.

The only sketch in this volume to have appeared originally in *Appletons' Journal* (October 4, 1873), "St. Clair Flats" contains some of Miss Woolson's most interesting early work, a view shared by her and expressed in a letter to Samuel Mather written in 1875: "I have all along cherished a special regard for 'St. Clair Flats,' and have felt troubled because no one else seemed to care for the poor thing; now here comes along a young man, for whose literary taste I have a sincere respect, and this delightful young man picks out my poor neglected sketch for special commendation!" (Benedict, II, 22-23).

In this piece, two men, one of whom narrates the story, visit the flats of the St. Clair River, near Detroit, to fish and hunt; and they find a place to stay with Waiting Samuel, an eloquent but uneducated religious fanatic whose religion is compounded of "a strange mixture of Jacob Boehmen, chiliastic dreams, Christianity, sun-worship, and modern spiritualism," and his wife Roxana, a native of Maine. Roxana tells her story to the visitors, and the reader becomes aware that Miss Woolson has deftly sketched a memorable character. Because of her great love for her husband, Roxana has given up her own name, her family, and her native heath. She is lonely and sometimes memories of the past overwhelm her, but she is steadfast in her faith in Samuel's "great gifts" (one cannot help thinking here of Deerslayer "Christian's gifts" and "white gifts") and in her love for him; and she does not seriously consider returning to the land of lost content. Thus, the author turns to contrast again in showing the differences between these two wedded for life, the one poetic and prophetic and the other prosaic and pathetic; yet these two accept their lot and neither complains of incompatibility.

The treatment of the background also adds distinction to this sketch. Miss Woolson is at her best in describing the natural features of the St. Clair Flats.

> The word "marsh" does not bring up a beautiful picture to the mind, and yet the reality was as beautiful as anything I have ever seen—an enchanted land, whose memory haunts me as an idea unwritten, a melody unsung, a picture unpainted, haunts the artist, and will not away. On each side and in front, as far as the eye could reach, stretched the low green land which was yet no land, intersected by hundreds of channels, narrow and broad, whose waters were green as their shores. In and out, now running into each other for a moment, now setting off each for himself again, these many channels flowed along with a rippling current; zigzag as they were, they never seemed to loiter, but, as if knowing just where they were going and what they had to do, they found time to take their own pleasant roundabout way, visiting the secluded households of their friends the flags, who, poor souls, must always stay at home. These currents were as clear as crystal, and green as the water-grasses that fringed their miniature shores. The bristling reeds, like companies of free-lances, rode boldly out here and there into

> the deeps, trying to conquer more territory for the grasses, but the currents were hard to conquer; they dismounted the free-lances, and flowed over their submerged heads; they beat them down with assaulting ripples; they broke their backs so effectually that the bravest had no spirit left, but trailed along, limp and bedraggled. And, if by chance the lances succeeded in stretching their forces across from one little shore to another, then the unconquered currents forced their way between the closely serried ranks of the enemy, and flowed on as gayly as ever, leaving the grasses sitting hopeless on the bank; for they needed solid ground for their delicate feet, these graceful ladies in green [306-7].[7]

"St. Clair Flats" is, on the whole, an interesting sketch which gives promise of better work to come.

The remaining sketches in the collections were all published first in the *Atlantic*.[8] Howells thought these three the "best in this book." Two of these—"Solomon" and "Wilhelmina"—are set in the Zoar Community in Ohio and are not strictly lake-country work. In his review of *Castle Nowhere,* Howells describes "Solomon" as

> a triumph of its kind—a novel kind, as simple as it is fresh. The Zoar Community, with its manners and customs, and that quaint mingling of earthy good-feeling and mild, coarse kindliness with forms of austere religious and social discipline, which seems to characterize all the peculiar German sectarians, has had the fortune to find an artist in the first who introduces us to its life. Solomon's character is studied with a delicate and courageous sympathy, which spares us nothing of his grotesqueness, and yet keenly touches us with his pathetic history. An even greater success of literary art is his poor, complaining wife, the faded parody of the idol of his young love, still beautiful in his eyes, and the inspiration of all his blind, unguided efforts in painting. His death, after the first instruction has revealed his powers to himself, is affectingly portrayed, without a touch of sentimentalistic insistence. It is a very complete and beautiful story [737].

In "Wilhelmina," Miss Woolson apparently described too accurately some of her originals at Zoar, for the publication of the piece disturbed people at the Community, as she acknowledged in a letter to Samuel Mather in 1875. "Some one sent me a New Philadelphia paper containing a savage article on 'Wilhelmina,' based upon the idea that my characters were all from life, and consequently 'the leathery woman' was the good Mrs. Beiter, the gardener's wife, etc., etc. Of course the article in the country paper was of no consequence, but I was distressed to think that perhaps the Beiters, always good friends of mine, thought so, too. I therefore wrote to Mr. Beiter telling him it was but a fancy sketch" (Benedict, II, 22).

Howells thought "Wilhelmina" "not quite so good" as "Solomon." The reason is not far to seek. Wilhelmina herself somehow fails to come alive, and her emotional attachment to her lover Gustav never seems quite real. The use of a detached observer-character to narrate the story also influences adversely the credibility and effectiveness of Wilhelmina as a character. In this instance, as Claude M. Simpson has pointed out in another connection, the "personality" of the narrator becomes a "formidable barrier between reader and scene." Despite these handicaps, Miss Woolson does manage, as Kern has maintained, to stimulate some sympathy in the reader for the plight of the "pathetic girl at the apathy of her erstwhile lover."

"The Lady of Little Fishing," the last story in the collection—though it had appeared concurrently with "Peter the Parson"—is in many ways also the best. The Lady is a beautiful Scottish missionary who appears suddenly one night among the rough trappers and hunters of Little Fishing, a camp on an island in Lake Superior, and whose beneficent influence on their lives reminds one of the "Luck's" impact on the miners of Harte's Roaring Camp. Almost as rapidly as her influence has waxed does it wane, when the men discover that she has fallen in love with one of their number (ironically, the only man there who is not in love with her); and thus, in Miss Woolson's sketch, "the problem of their unnaturally restrained behavior," as Simpson puts it, is resolved "by the strictly human device of disenchantment, where Harte resorted to chance calamity."[9]

Pattee, in his *Development of the American Short Story*, compares Miss Woolson's story with Harte's and then generalizes briefly on her artistry in the short story:

> 'The Lady of Little Fishing,' . . . greatly surpassed in short-story art Harte's 'Luck of Roaring Camp.' The motif of Harte's piece centers about the abnormality of a group of men isolated completely from all feminine and domestic influences and the grotesque extremes to which such a group may go when such an element appears suddenly among them. . . . Miss Woolson does all that Harte does, and then she adds a touch that makes her

> work a model short story, as Harte's is not. All the men but one are in love with the Lady, and she is forced to choose one from among them. She chooses Mitchell, who refuses her absolutely, and then explains himself to the amazed group whom she had rejected: '*I* never gave in to her influence; *I* was never under her thumb. *I* was the only man in Little Fishing who cared nothing for her.' 'And that is the secret of *her* liking,' murmured the Doctor. 'O woman! woman! the same the world over!'
> This is the real motif of the story; not the mere grotesqueness of an abnormal situation presented merely for entertainment and wonder. The story is not finished when the reader has read it: it becomes with him a haunting suspicion, a peep into the heart of life [255].

Pattee concludes that Miss Woolson "must be rated with James and Aldrich as a strong influence toward more careful short-story workmanship at a moment when such influence peculiarly was needed" (255). There is little one may add to this critical and historical appraisal today. In this story Miss Woolson's insight has touched upon the universal, and she has bettered the work of one of her masters.

As a whole, *Castle Nowhere* (1875) is a good first book. In comparison with Sarah Orne Jewett's *Deephaven* (1877) and Mary N. Murfree's *In the Tennessee Mountains* (1884), to choose only two titles of similar quality from among the first books of Miss Woolson's feminine contemporaries, *Castle Nowhere* holds its own pretty well. In treatment and development of character and in the realization of background and locale, these early sketches give promise of the work to come. They are pioneer work, a fact one should not forget in assessing their value. "The ground is new," Howells wrote in the *Atlantic* in 1875, "and Miss Woolson gathers from it a harvest out of which the grain had not been threshed long ago." That the granaries were later to be filled to overflowing from the work of many harvesters should not obscure the fact that Miss Woolson made a distinct contribution in this book and others to follow both in local-color fiction and in analysis of character.

II *Rodman the Keeper*

Miss Woolson's second volume of short fiction, *Rodman the Keeper: Southern Sketches* (1880), contains several of her best stories and is, as a whole, certainly one of her best books. As one may recall, Mrs. Woolson's health demanded a more salubrious climate than that offered by either New York or New England, so the mother and her two daughters spent much of each year from 1873 to 1879 (when Mrs. Woolson died) in Virginia, the Carolinas, Georgia, and Florida. Thus a new territory was opened to Miss Woolson, and she took advantage of it in both short story and novel.

During the last half of the decade of the 1870's she wrote and published a number of sketches with Southern characters and settings. As early as September, 1877, James R. Osgood offered to bring out a collection of her Southern pieces, though five of the sketches which appeared eventually in the book had not yet been published and Miss Woolson was anxious to have her unfinished novel come out before a second book of sketches was ready for the press. On May 5, 1878, she wrote Stedman that her novel was finished; but for some reason, negotiations with Osgood fell through and the novel went to Harper and the short stories to D. Appleton. Contrary to her original plans, the novel appeared after the collection of ten pieces selected from among those that had appeared in the *Atlantic, Appletons'*, the *Galaxy, Harper's, Lippincott's Magazine,* and *Scribner's Monthly.*[10]

"Rodman the Keeper," the title piece, appeared first in the *Atlantic* in March, 1877. The story, which takes place in the South in the early days of Reconstruction, concerns John Rodman, a former Federal officer who is now the keeper of a national cemetery;[11] Ward De Rosset, a former Confederate soldier who lies critically wounded in the ruins of his home; Bettina Ward, De Rosset's intended bride who cannot forget the feelings stirred up by the war; and Pomp, an old Negro who remains faithful to his former master despite the outcome of the war. There are, it may readily be observed, materials for sentiment and reconciliation here, but Miss Woolson has firm control over the pathetic potentialities inherent in her sketch. To be sure, Rodman nurses De Rosset to the best of his ability, but neither falls on the neck of the other as a result; and Bettina Ward only late in the piece, after De Rosset has died, wavers in her harsh opinion of Yankees. Even at the end, when Rodman makes the generous gesture of buying some of the "greenery" from the old De Rosset place that is now owned by a "Maine man," the matter is treated ironically, not sentimentally. "One can only be thankful," Jay B.

Hubbell has remarked, "that the tragic theme was handled by a sincere artist like Miss Woolson and not by one of the numerous sentimental writers who would have devised an intersectional romance culminating in the marriage of a proud Southern beauty to a Northern hero in blue."[12]

"Rodman" was well received by the critics. In a letter of February 24, 1877, to Samuel Mather, Miss Woolson described her reaction to the attention given her sketch:

> As I think you are interested in the subject, I will mention how much gratification I have had over the reception of 'Rodman the Keeper' in the last *Atlantic. The Tribune* (semi-weekly) copied it entire, the *Times* gave it a flattering notice, and from many quarters I have received letters full of pleasure. Last but not least, it called out a letter from a well-known firm [presumably Harper & Brothers] asking whether it would not be possible for me to send *all* I wrote to their house? That they would gladly take every line and pay as much as any other house had ever paid, and, in fact, I could set my own price [Benedict, II, 23-24].

What more flattering notice could an aspiring young writer seek?

The second sketch in the collection, "Sister St. Luke," had appeared first in the *Galaxy* in April, 1877, only a month after "Rodman" had come out in the *Atlantic*. The scene is set in Florida where two Northern men have come on vacation. (It is perhaps not too much to say at this point that in the matter of placing Northerners in a Southern locale in order to study and describe the effect of the culture and scene on them, Miss Woolson anticipated her later device of putting Americans in a European scene for much the same reasons.) Sister St. Luke is a frail and ill member of an order that no longer wants her. She has been sent to live with Pedro Gonsalvez, a Minorcan light-housekeeper, and his New England wife, Melvyna Sawyer. There she is met by George Carrington and Andrew Keith, two "city men" from the North who have come to the island to rest. In the course of time, Carrington and Keith join forces with Melvyna in trying to bring Sister St. Luke back to health. Finally, Keith sends money to the convent so that Sister St. Luke may return; and then, after a terrible tornado has left the two men clinging to a reef, the little nun saves them by sailing a boat to their rescue despite her fear of both water and boat. On the next day Sister St. Luke goes back to the convent.

The characters contribute most to the effectiveness of this sketch. Pedro Gonsalvez, the indolent Minorcan whose only reply to argument is to smile "as sweetly and as softly as molasses"; Melvyna Sawyer, the New England alien in a "sunny land" she does not understand or appreciate but whose experience there has tended to round the sharp edges of her Puritan character without changing it fundamentally; Carrington and Keith, the visitors, whose concern for Sister St. Luke is at one and the same time a revelation of their characters—all these are carefully sketched; but it is the little nun who is the triumph of the piece. She is gentle and sentimental, yet her character is not developed sentimentally; and she represents the best qualities of any religious order; that is, she is kind and thinks of others before herself, she is brave and courageous in the face of dangers that frighten her, and she possesses a simple and abiding faith in her order and church that moves even Melvyna Sawyer, the strict Calvinist. In commenting on the work as a whole, one may properly follow the late Arthur Hobson Quinn in stressing the "breadth" of Miss Woolson's understanding of races and religions not her own and in suggesting also that her well-known sympathy for the ill-used and downtrodden is displayed at its best in this story.[13]

Like "Sister St. Luke," the scene in "Miss Elisabetha" is set in Florida, and one of the chief characters (in this instance the lady of the title herself) is from the North.[14] Miss Elisabetha is an elderly spinster of Dutch extraction who has come south to care for Theodore, the young son of her old sweetheart Petrus Oesterand and a Florida mother of Spanish descent. In her concern for "Doro," Miss Elisabetha overprotects him and thus opens the way to an unfortunate marriage with a local Minorcan beauty whose family connections (to the old lady's mind) are hardly proper for such a match. Nevertheless, Doro and Catalina manage to live happily if carelessly and indolently, and Miss Elisabetha, despite her standards and her misgivings, remains faithful to her charge to the end.

Once again the characters make the sketch. Cécile Kernadi, the famous prima donna who wishes to supervise and sponsor an operatic career for Doro, is one of Miss Woolson's best minor characterizations. And the scene in which Cécile is confronted by Miss Elisabetha, who refuses to give up the boy, is a deft dramatic revelation of the singer's character as well as the old spinster's. Miss Elisabetha herself is a skillful realization of the old-fashioned lady and old maid whose one romantic attachment—fruitless though it may have been in one sense—has blossomed into an emotion as deep and lasting as mother-love itself.[15] It is not hard to understand why Miss Woolson considered this story one of her "favorites," though it is more difficult to accept H. H. Boyesen's verdict that "Miss Elisabetha" is the "most artistically complete" piece in this collection. Doro's failure to be anything more than a shadowy representation of a typically overprotected young man mars the artistic completeness of the sketch. Otherwise, one may well appreciate its qualities of excellence.

One finds even less to cavil about in "Old Gardiston," surely one of Miss Woolson's finest stories.[16] The title of the piece is also the name of a house in South Carolina that, in its relationship to the family which owns it, reminds the reader, in one sense at least, of Poe's House of Usher. In the old Gardiston house, in the reduced circumstances brought about by defeat in war and by poverty in war's aftermath, live young Miss Gardis Duke and her elderly cousin, Copeland Gardiston, the last members of the Gardiston family. A company of Northern troops under the command of Captain David Newell is ordered to camp in the area. On one occasion Captain Newell and his men save the house from an attack by Negroes, and in response to this act, Miss Duke, though it goes against the grain, invites Newell and his second in command to dinner. In the end, with the help of Newell (and after the death of Cousin Copeland) Gardis Duke sells the house, but before she can move, it symbolically burns to the ground; and the last of the Gardistons accepts the romantic overtures of Captain Newell.[17]

Thus the inevitable beautiful Southern belle is brought to the arms of the gallant Federal officer, but there is more to this tale than the shopworn reconciliation theme, which was, of course, not so "shopworn" in 1876 when "Old Gardiston" appeared in the April issue of *Harper's*. The author's emphasis is focused on the Southern characters, each of whom she sketches with understanding and discrimination. Their foibles and their virtues are examined, and the traditional Southern pride in family (and genealogy) is gently satirized; but a good part of the merit of this story lies in Miss Woolson's respect for the South Carolina character both as abstraction and as reality.[18] Alexander Cowie has recently characterized the piece as "an almost perfect short story" and remarked on Miss Woolson's capacity to bring out the "poignant suffering of the South." "Old Gardiston" is worthy of attention as a sympathetic and knowledgeable treatment, by one of the victorious side, of a proud people in defeat. Few of those who shared Miss Woolson's Republican principles in the 1870's were able to be so fair to the fallen enemy.

To some nineteenth-century critics, "The South Devil" was one of Constance Woolson's "finest achievements." A reviewer in *Scribner's*, for example, thought that this sketch contained the "best writing" in the volume; and Howells, writing later in *Harper's*, was particularly impressed by the swamp background:[19]

> The landscape is apt to grow sentient under her touch, which in the portrayal of that beautiful and deadly Florida swamp in 'The South Devil' is really life-giving: the wicked, brilliant thing becomes animate. In this a writer who has since evolved for herself one of the most interesting phases of realism is romantic, but her epoch is distinctly marked by her forbearance in another respect: she does not extort an allegory from the malign morass, . . . nor suggest a psychical significance in it. . . . It is a merely animal life which 'The South Devil' lives.

The swamp is indeed a living thing, and Miss Woolson makes effective use of its paradoxical life-giving and life-taking qualities. In fact, the swamp so dominates this sketch that the characters are dwarfed by it; the emphasis on tone, color, and atmosphere is all-pervasive. Even the identification of one of the chief characters with the swamp seems only to stress the power and influence of "the beautiful, deadly South Devil":

> They passed under the gray and solemn cypresses, rising without branches to an enormous height, their far foliage hidden by the moss, which hung down thickly in long flakes, diffusing the sunshine and making it silvery like mist; in the silver swung the air-plants, great cream-colored disks, and wands of scarlet, crowded with little buds, blossoms that looked like butterflies, and blossoms that looked like humming-birds, and little dragon-heads with grinning faces. Then they came to the region of the palms; these shot up, slender and graceful, and leaned over the stream, the great aureum-ferns growing on their trunks high in the air. Beneath was a firmer soil than in the domain of the cypresses, and here grew a mat of little flowers, each less than a quarter of an inch wide, close together, pink, blue, scarlet,

> yellow, purple, but never white, producing a hue singularly rich, owing to the absence of that colorless color which man ever mingles with his floral combinations, and strangely makes sacred alike to the bridal and to death. Great vines ran up the palms, knotted themselves, and came down again, hand over hand, wreathed in little fresh leaves of exquisite green. Birds with plumage of blush-rose pink flew slowly by; also some with scarlet wings, and the jeweled paroquets. The great Savannah cranes stood on the shore, and did not stir as the boat moved by. And, as the spring was now in its prime, the alligators showed their horny heads above water, and climbed awkwardly out on the bank. . . . The air was absolutely still; no breeze reached these blossoming aisles; each leaf hung motionless. The atmosphere was hot, and heavy with perfumes. It was the heart of the swamp, a riot of intoxicating, steaming, swarming, fragrant, beautiful, tropical life, without man to make or mar it. All the world was once so, before man was made [173-74].

Thus the sketch has, in reality, much of the quality of a prose tone poem, and in this sense differs from the others in this collection. Yet as Quinn has pointed out in *American Fiction*: "The way [Miss Woolson] establishes the mystical relation between the great swamp and Carl, the young musician who hears the harmonies the swamp sings only to him, and who cannot keep away from it though it may mean death to him, reveals her great power of understanding the relations of place and human character" (334).

"In the Cotton Country," a sketch brought out originally in the issue of *Appletons'* for April 29, 1876, provides in its stress on character and lack of concern with background a fine contrast to "The South Devil." Miss Woolson makes skillful use of a double first-person point of view in this work, though actually the narrative is unfolded through a Northern observer's recounting of a Southern woman's trials and tribulations during the war and after, as told to her in a modified dramatic monologue fashion.

Judith Cotesworth Kinsolving, a descendant of an old South Carolina plantation family and the widow of a Confederate soldier,[20] describes in a straightforward way her experiences during the war and its aftermath. She has lost everything: her husband, father, two brothers, a sister-in-law, servants, and possessions; and, after the war, she has lived as a poverty-stricken poor white in the area where she formerly lived in splendor. The sketch is, as Kern has pointed out with good reason, "drably realistic," for it is, according to the author herself, "a story of fact." "It is true," she once wrote, "every word of it, save the names given" (Kern, 73). Despite this assertion, "In the Cotton Country" is easily one of the best examples of Miss Woolson's well-known sympathy for those in the postwar South who had lost everything in the disaster of defeat. Howells was aware of this in 1887 when he observed in the February issue of *Harper's* that the pieces collected in *Rodman* achieved "vastly more than their aesthetic interest by eternizing that moment of heart-break and irreconciliation in the South when its women began to realize all their woe and loss through the defeat of their section in the war" (482).

"Felipa," which appeared in *Lippincott's* in June, 1876, shortly after "In the Cotton Country" had been brought out by *Appletons'*, is primarily a character sketch of a "small, dark-skinned, yellow-eyed child, the offspring of the ocean and the heats, tawny, lithe and wild, shy yet fearless" who lives with her Minorcan grandparents on the coast of Florida. Into Felipa's young life (she is "nearly twelve" years old) enter three persons from the North: Catherine, the artist-narrator; Christine, her beautiful companion; and Edward Bowne, Christine's suitor. Though Catherine cares more for her, Felipa gives her heart to Christine and Edward; and, when she learns that they are about to leave and be married, she first tries to take her own life and then Edward's. She fails in both attempts, and the visitors depart quickly, leaving Felipa to absorb the sad and bitter experience of frustrated young love.

H. H. Boyesen, the Norwegian-American novelist and educator, in his review of *Rodman* in *Scribner's* in August, 1880, noted a single "lapse from psychological realism" in "Felipa" and then concluded his remarks on this tale: "The passionate attachment of the yellow little savage to the beautiful, fair-skinned Northern lady, her hunger for praise and her resolute despair at being repulsed, are in themselves very pathetic, and the pathos is nowise weakened by the half-humorous manner in which the story is related." One may add to this comment that Miss Woolson's understanding of and insight into the juvenile mind is impressive evidence of her knowledge of human nature in general and that, as Boyesen suggests, the interpretation of

Felipa may indeed be based on a "charmingly elaborated sketch from some living original."

Another sketch that may have been "elaborated" from the original is that of "'Bro'," which appeared first in *Appletons'* in November, 1878. Ambrose (Bro) Cranch is a "rawboned" and "nondescript" sawmiller from the "upcountry" of a Southern state. Though "simple" and "inoffensive," he manages through the sale of one of his inventions to give his friends, Mrs. Manning and her daughter Marion, the things each wants most in life—security in the case of the former and the husband of her choice in the case of the latter. Thus "Bro," who loves Marion himself, makes it possible (without revealing to her his own feelings) for her to marry another man, thereby placing himself among those characters in Miss Woolson's fiction who sacrifice their own desires in behalf of someone they love. Nor is "Bro" the only male to do so. Old Fog denies himself in caring for Silver in "Castle Nowhere," and David Newell all but gives up Gardis Duke in "Old Gardiston." "Bro's" sacrifice is greater than these because he not only gives up the woman he loves without telling her that he loves her or that he has helped her, but, in order to make his assistance most effective, he denies himself the pleasure of having members of the community know of the success of his invention. On the whole, though "Bro" is not unbelievable as a character, his completely selfless actions may make him appear rather quixotic to modern readers.[21]

The next sketch in the collection, "King David," also contains a somewhat quixotic central character, but the author's handling of this character and his situation makes her treatment of "Bro" appear a bit naïve. "King David" is a convincing study of the difficulties experienced by an idealistic New England schoolmaster with the "almost hopelessly improvident and lazy" Southern Negro freedmen he tries to teach.[22] David King, a young abolitionist teacher from New Hampshire, comes south after the war with the laudable purpose of educating the freedmen and raising them out of their poverty and ignorance; but the slothful and easy-going blacks of Jubilee Town do not respond to his efforts to teach them the rudiments of reading and writing. Nor does he succeed any better when he finally appeals for help to Harnett Ammerton, a representative of the old planter class who resents and disagrees with King's whole approach to the teaching of the former slaves. In the final analysis King fails in his mission because he does not understand the Negro and because even after five months in the South (though he believes in the equality of the races) he still "shrinks from personal contact with the other race" and goes about his work from a sense of "duty, not liking."[23]

"King David" succeeds as a work of fiction because, as one critic has remarked, it contains no "exaggeration" and because it reveals on the one hand a breadth of knowledge and a sympathetic understanding of a situation that few Northern observers could approach and on the other an objectivity that few Southern commentators possessed with regard to the particular problem. Miss Woolson's point of view in the story becomes all the more remarkable when one remembers that she was a native of New Hampshire and a staunch Unionist. That the work possesses more than a passing topical pertinence should be clear to the modern reader, for its point, as Hubbell has described it—that "good intentions are not enough for those who plan to make over the life of a region which they do not fully understand" (*SAL,* 737)—is still relevant in the self-styled Atomic Age.

The last piece in *Rodman,* "Up in the Blue Ridge," appeared first in *Appletons'* in August, 1878, less than six months after *Scribner's* had brought out "King David." As the title suggests, the setting is in the "mountains of the middle South" (Miss Woolson in a letter identifies the area as that of Asheville and its environs), though in this instance, as in others, some of the chief characters are from the North. Actually there is not a single important character in this work who is a genuine mountaineer. In many respects Brother Bethuel Head, the Methodist missionary in the Ellerby area, resembles the mountain circuit riders in some of Mary N. Murfree's later work, but Head is originally from the low country.

The action is mainly concerned with the efforts of Stephen Wainwright, a wealthy self-made Northern businessman (in one sense an early study of Horace Chase), to help, at first, and, later, to win the hand of Honor Dooris, the attractive niece of Colonel Eliot, head of a branch of a well-known "low-country" family that has moved to the mountains. Because of his interest in Honor, Wainwright contributes financial assistance to the economy of the village. Finally, even when he thinks that she loves Richard Eliot, the Colonel's oldest son and a member of a band of "whisky-men," Wainwright seeks to help Eliot escape capture by Federal troops, though his efforts to do this and remain a law-abiding citizen are not entirely successful. When Eliot escapes and Wainwright discovers that Honor loves John Royce, he bows to the inevitable and returns to Adelaide Kellinger, his friend and confidante who has been in love with him for years.

"Up in the Blue Ridge" is a bit too long (it runs to sixty-three pages in book form), but it contains good character sketches of Wainwright, Adelaide, and Brother Bethuel and some shrewd analyses of the motivations of Wainwright and Adelaide under certain circumstances. The mountain background is also neatly done, and there are deft touches regarding Southern life and culture, especially in regard to Southern literary taste.[24] In the final analysis, "Up in the Blue Ridge" lacks the concentration and understanding of "Old Gardiston" and "King David," the dramatic contrasts of "Rodman the Keeper," and the all-pervasive tone and atmosphere of "The South Devil." It is a good sketch, but despite its early treatment of the Southern mountains in fiction, "Up in the Blue Ridge" is not so significant a piece of work as the stories just mentioned.

Rodman the Keeper, on the whole, contains work that is mature in insight, that is warm (and yet not excessively sentimental) with sympathetic understanding of a region not the author's own, and that is filled with knowledge not bred in the bone but acquired and expressed with reasonable objectivity. On this last point, Miss Woolson wrote H. H. Boyesen from Lucerne on August 9 [1880?]: "That you call the book 'convincing' gives me much gratification, because I tried hard to be accurate. It is much easier, I think, to imagine than to simply describe; and I called myself back many times, when at work on these sketches, from tempting exaggeration and fancies, to plain fact."[25]

A critic in *Harper's* for June, 1880, generously characterized Miss Woolson's artistry in this collection of stories:

> She is a conscientious and true artist. Thoroughly loyal to art, she carefully elaborates the minor accessories, without sacrificing vigor or originality to mere finish; and the general effect of her stories is enhanced by her skillful blending of color and her admirably balanced arrangement of actors and scenery. Intensely realistic, she is never a literal copyist, but her pictures of real scenes and characters are invariably invested with an added beauty and picturesqueness through the agency of a fertile and

trained imagination. This union of realism and idealism insures variety as well as grace to her compositions, since nature constantly suggests new and varying types and phases, and fancy as constantly gilds them with what Shakespeare calls its 'heavenly alchymy'. . . . The sketches . . . collected in this volume place their author in the first rank of writers in this line; nay, we know of no writer, English or American, whose short stories are so rich in description, so strong in their delineations of character, so opulent in narrative or dramatic interest, and so truly poetic in their settings and surroundings [152].

This praise may appear somewhat fulsome to readers of the mid-twentieth century, but it was close to the mark in 1880. Even today there is some justice in the assertions concerning characters and background and poetic imagination. In this instance, it is well to let Henry James have the last word on his friend's work. In *Partial Portraits,* he remarked that *Rodman the Keeper* was "full of interesting artistic work" and then observed:

As the fruit of a remarkable minuteness of observation and tenderness of feeling on the part of one who evidently did not glance and pass, but lingered and analysed, they have a high value, especially when regarded in the light of the *voicelessness* of the conquered and reconstructed South. Miss Woolson strikes the reader as having a compassionate sense of this pathetic dumbness. . . . She loves the whole region, and no daughter of the land could have handled its peculiarities more indulgently, or communicated to us more of the sense of close observation and intimate knowledge [179-80].[26]

III *The Front Yard*

The Front Yard and Other Italian Stories (1895) was published posthumously, though the House of Harper, as Miss Woolson informed Samuel Mather not long before she died, had suggested that she select some of her Italian stories for a new volume. She apparently did this, and the result is a book containing six stories published in the period 1882-92 in *Harper's,* the *Atlantic,* and the *Century.* Thus *The Front Yard* reprints "The Street of the Hyacinth" (1882) and "In Venice" (1882), two of Constance Woolson's early stories dealing with Americans in Italy; and "A Christmas Party" (1892), one of her latest tales of this sort. With the exception of the title piece and "The Street of the

Hyacinth," the stories in this collection do not quite measure up to the best ones in *Castle Nowhere* and *Rodman the Keeper*. This is not to suggest that her work in this vein is not good; on the contrary, the point is rather that her stories with American backgrounds are even better.[27]

"The Front Yard," a contribution to *Harper's* in December, 1888, contains one of the best character studies Miss Woolson ever wrote, that of Prudence Wilkin, a New England woman of rural background and little education who goes to Italy as the companion and attendant of a wealthy cousin. When the cousin dies, Prudence decides to remain in Assisi and marry Antonio Guadagni, a waiter who has discovered that she has saved up a bit of money and makes it his business to offer her the only romance she has ever known. Going to her new home after the marriage, Prudence discovers that it contains eight children as well as Antonio's first wife's grandmother and uncle, to say nothing of an ugly "cowshed" in what should be the front yard.

For the next sixteen years (Antonio dies after the first year) Prudence gives herself to supporting this family and to dreaming of the day when she can acquire enough money to have the cowshed taken away and to plant flowers and bushes in her own "front yard." Each time her savings begin to mount up, one of the children needs money until finally, when after months of saving she has the required amount, her favorite among them, Jo Vanny (Giovanni), steals it and runs away. Months later Prudence, whose health is now broken by years of hard work, is discovered by an American tourist who cares for the old woman in her last days. The cowshed is removed and a fence and flowers make the small area the "front yard" of Prudence's dream; but, pleased though she is, her last thought is of Giovanni.

The writer of a review of the book in the *Critic* for December 28, 1895, praised this story highly. "The story is a brilliant piece of genre-painting," he remarks, "executed by an artist who understood her subject to the heart. A strange combination of humor and pathos," he continues, "it contains much the finest work in the volume; it is the one story that shows originality of invention without the least straining after effect, the only one in which the method is entirely adequate to the idea." One may agree, with perhaps a reservation or two: (1) the conclusion seems a bit contrived and not quite so inevitable as one might desire in such a work of fiction; and (2) the method and idea are also adequately related in "The Street of the Hyacinth."

A word should also be said about "The Front Yard's" place in Miss Woolson's fiction of international incident. Some of her work of this sort certainly belongs to the school of James and Howells (though in this field, as in her local-color work on the lake country and on the South, she is something of a pioneer); but this story offers a change in approach and emphasis from the work of James and Howells. In "The Front Yard" the central character is not only a humble member of society, but the whole point of view is focused on that character and, therefore, on a different level of society from that usually treated in international-episode fiction. This change in the angle of vision provides new insight into the usual comparisons drawn between the two cultures of America and Europe. Prudence Wilkin does not know anything about Italian painting or art; in fact she is not aware that some of Giotto's best frescoes are in Assisi (she is not even aware of Giotto!). She has come to Italy to perform one duty, and she remains to perform another. This does not mean that she has no taste for beauty, for her dream is to have a New England style "front yard" with a "new paling fence," a gate, currant bushes, and flower beds of "bachelor's-buttons, Chiny-asters, lady's-slippers, and pinks." Thus her taste for beauty is for the natural arrangements of the New World and not for the artistic wonders of the Old. In this, too, "The Front Yard" represents a departure from the work of James and Howells.

On the whole, one is inclined to assign this piece a high place in the canon of Miss Woolson's short fiction. Prudence Wilkin is a memorable characterization, and the contrast between New England ways and Italian peasant ways is skillfully developed and exploited, to say nothing of the more general contrast presented between the New World and the Old. Moreover, the theme of self-sacrifice that is so important in Miss Woolson's work is treated with restraint and discrimination. As Pattee pointed out many years ago in the *Cambridge History of American Literature,* stories like "The Front Yard" "are constructed of the materials of life itself. One cannot forget them" (II, 382).

Though it appeared in *Harper's* in October, 1888, two months before "The Front Yard," "Neptune's Shore" appears immediately after the title piece in this collection. Not so good a story as "The Front Yard," it does contain at least one character who approaches the quality of Prudence Wilkin. Mrs. Azubah Ash, the uneducated but doting mother of the clever and wealthy John Ash, does not in this work (as does Prudence in her piece) command the center of the stage until near the end. The story is, strictly speaking, not hers but her son's, and this is one of its chief defects.

The scene is established in the area of Salerno-Paestum, where a group of Americans are visiting the Greek temples. The framework of the action involves a love triangle. John Ash, a willful man of strong temperament, pays court to Mrs. Pauline Graham, a beautiful young widow and the niece of the wealthy Mrs. Octavia Preston. Being something of a flirt, Mrs. Graham encourages Ash's attentions until she becomes interested in Griff Carew, a young American architect and the mentor of Arthur Abercrombie, Mrs. Preston's nephew. Ash becomes enraged and finally shoots and critically wounds Carew after Mrs. Graham refuses to break an engagement she has made with the architect to go to Naples. A tornado follows the shooting, and Ash and his mother escape from the others. With Carew at the point of death, Mrs. Ash suddenly returns to announce that John has taken his own life and to express her hope that Carew will live. Dominated by her headstrong son for years, she has at last, with his death, come into her own; now she no longer need fear for him the consequences of his impulsive, unruly actions.

Besides those nice touches of characterization in Mrs. Ash, there are one or two others in this tale. Isabella, Pauline Graham's old-maid cousin, is one. She has six hundred "well bred" dollars a year, and though she disapproves of Mrs. Ash's "vulgar affluence," Isabella does not hesitate to inform John's mother that Pauline is a "sad, sad flirt." There are also some shrewd insights into the character of Octavia Preston, the self-willed old matriarch who does not "care much about the future" because her "tests" are "those of the past" and whose "gracious" reception of Griff Carew is based not on the young architect's charm but rather on the "certificate" of her own acquaintance with Griff's mother.

The members of the romantic triangle, however, are not among Miss Woolson's best portraits. Ash is a bit too melodramatic for twentieth-century tastes; Pauline Graham is not adequately developed; and Carew's character is hardly more than sketchily suggested. Nor is the background as effectively realized as in other stories, despite Miss Woolson's enthusiasm for the ruins of

Paestum.[28] On the whole, "Neptune's Shore" is a more conventional treatment of Americans in a continental setting than is "The Front Yard," and the melodramatic quality of Ash's actions adversely affects the late development in his mother's character. As a reviewer in the *Critic* observes, the "tragedy" in this tale "does not touch one deeply."

"The Pink Villa" appeared in the November *Harper's*, one month after "Neptune's Shore" and one month before the publication of "The Front Yard." The villa itself is a "delicious nest" crowning "one of the perpendicular cliffs of Sorrento" and "overlooking what is perhaps the most beautiful expanse of water in the world—the Bay of Naples," an area Miss Woolson had visited and admired in the early 1880's. The chief characters are, with one exception, Americans of wealth and position and therefore in keeping with much international-episode fiction. Mrs. Fanny Churchill is a fine characterization of an American mother who has expatriated herself in order to capture a proper European husband of rank for her daughter. She is almost successful in this venture, and Eva is satisfied with young Pierre Verneuil, the son of a wealthy Belgian noble, until Horace Bartholomew, an old friend of Mrs. Churchill's, brings David Rod to tea. Rod, a native of Florida where his father had been a Methodist missionary in "the early days," is a hard-working young man on his way up, though he is yet far from being rich and is relatively uncultured—his attendance at a "forlorn little Methodist college somewhere in Georgia" notwithstanding. Eva falls in love with Rod; and, despite her mother's strong objections, she marries him and goes to Florida, leaving Mrs. Churchill to contemplate the ruin of her grandiose plans for her daughter (and for herself) and to anticipate a bleak future in which she can no longer treat Eva as a "hot-house flower" and act as her "only protector."

Many of the characters in this story of Americans in Italy are treated conventionally. There is, on the one hand, the American who imitates English manners and dress; on the other, the American who is not sure that Europe is up to the best that the New World has to offer. There are, however, at least two departures from the usual. Mrs. Churchill's concern for her daughter's future is subtly developed as being a self-centered solicitude for her own welfare; and David Rod is carefully characterized as a self-made Southerner who would seldom be content to let others do his work while he lolled on the gallery sipping a cool julep. As far as Miss Woolson's work is concerned, "The Pink Villa" is a variation on the theme of self-sacrifice that appears so often in her fiction.

"The Street of the Hyacinth," which first appeared in the *Century* for May and June, 1882, is the longest story in this collection. It places Americans in a Roman background. Ethelinda Faith ("Ettie") Macks, a naïve young painter from Tuscolee Falls, a town in the American West, comes to Rome to seek the advice and supervision of Raymond Noel, an American expatriate art critic and writer. Without desiring to spend much time on her and yet intrigued by her flattering opinion of his aesthetic judgment, he sends her to Horace Jackson, an English painter who is among the best teachers in Rome, though Miss Macks insists that she visit the galleries with Noel himself.

Thereafter Noel finds time occasionally to take her to one of the galleries, but the pressure of his own social engagements and work keeps him from seeing much of her, and a trip to Paris and London and Egypt takes him away from Rome for almost two years. When he returns, he discovers that she has given up painting and opened up a "day-school" in her apartment. Feeling that he has let her down in some way, he sets out to "try to atone" for the past, and ends up by falling in love with her. Misunderstanding the sincerity of the proposal that follows, she refuses Noel, though she has loved him for some time already. After this rejection, he refrains from visiting her, and she returns to Tuscolee to nurse her brother in his last illness. While she is in America, Noel regularly visits Ettie's mother Mrs. Spurr, a garrulous and uncultured old woman whose diction and manners are not adequate to the demands made by Roman society. When Ettie returns to Rome and discovers that Noel has been kind to her mother from the best of motives and that her apartment on the Street of the Hyacinth is to be demolished as part of a public works project, she finally gives in to Noel, and, together with Mrs. Spurr, they prepare for a new life in the Eternal City.

"The Street of the Hyacinth" is similar in several ways to " 'Miss Grief'," one of Miss Woolson's best uncollected tales (see note 27). In both stories the chief male character is an American expatriate writer and critic who is appealed to for help by an inexperienced American female artist. These naïve females are alike in the slight resemblance they bear to the young American admirer of Neil Paraday in James's "The Death of the Lion" (1894), but they are different in two ways: Ettie Macks has no artistic talent and "Miss Grief" has; and, in the second place, Ettie finds her fulfillment in a marriage with her mentor, whereas "Miss Grief" finds hers in her work. Both stories contain, moreover, other marks of resemblance to James's fiction. The narrator in "Miss Grief" and Noel both suggest certain Jamesian qualities of aesthetic sophistication; indeed, each may have been in part modelled on James himself, since Miss Woolson spent much time with her friend in the galleries and drawing rooms of Italy in the early 1880's. And, as Kern and Richardson have both suggested, there is also something of the method of James in the telling of these tales.

"The Street of the Hyacinth," however, has something to offer in its own right. The careful development of the chief characters and the sure sketching of the background reveal the hand of a mature artist at work. Ettie Macks is a convincing portrait of an inexperienced young woman who (without an awareness of the cost) expects miracles to happen and who lives to find that, though they may not appear when one expects them, this does not necessarily mean they do not occur at all. Raymond Noel is just the right balance between the dilettante and the man of principle whose concern for another leads him to a new maturity. And Mrs. Spurr, though only lightly sketched, is a delightful picture of an uneducated American mother who is out of her element in Rome but whose innate strength of character nevertheless provides the right antidote to her social inadequacy.

The old street itself is graphically described:

> It was a street in Rome—narrow, winding, not over-clean. Two vehicles meeting there could pass only by grazing the doors and windows on either side, after the usual excited whip-cracking and shouts which make the new-comer imagine, for his first day or two, that he is proceeding at a perilous speed through the sacred city of the soul.
>
> But two vehicles did not often meet in the street of the Hyacinth. It was not a thoroughfare, not even a convenient connecting link; it skirted the back of the Pantheon, the old buildings on either side rising so high against the blue that the sun never came down lower than the fifth line of windows, and looking up from the pavement was like looking up from the bottom of a well. There was no foot-walk, of course; even if

> there had been one no one would have used it, owing to the easy custom of throwing from the windows a few ashes and other light trifles for the city refuse-carts, instead of carrying them down the long stairs to the door below. They must be in the street at an appointed hour, must they not? Very well, then—there they were; no one but an unreasonable foreigner would dream of objecting [137].

As a whole, "The Street of the Hyacinth" is a good piece of work. Since it has little plot and therefore small need for such devices as tension, suspense, and denouement, it has the quality of a leisurely sketch that introduces its characters in an appropriate Old World setting and allows them to grow within the context of a dramatic contrast between the new and the old, between innocence and experience. The author's successful depiction of this contrast gives the work its quality of distinction.

The remaining two stories in this volume both contain Venetian backgrounds. The first of these, "A Christmas Party," came out in *Harper's* in December, 1892; it was the last among the six pieces to appear in a magazine. Another story of Americans in Italy, it possesses an element of excitement and suspense that one seldom finds in Miss Woolson's short fiction. As Richardson has pointed out, it is "the closest approach to a crime mystery" she ever wrote.

Peter Senter, the American consul in Venice, is in some respects a typical successful man of large fortune who refuses even to learn to speak the language of the country in which he serves (the "vice-consul," he avers, can attend to "business matters"), for he thinks it "unmasculine to have a polyglot tongue." His sister Barbara presides over his household and commands his retinue of servants, of whom Carmela, the assistant housekeeper, Ercole, the chief gondolier, and Giorgio, the chef, are important to the development of the narrative.

The action in the story centers around a Christmas party given by the consul in honor of his friends and of the American tourists in Venice. At the party a man disguised as a clown and introduced by Carmela to Miss Senter does tricks and entertains the children. Later it is discovered that the clown is not Ercole as planned but rather Carmela's son, a murderer, and that the assistant housekeeper is not all she seemed to be: a prim and proper middle-aged jewel of a servant. In the ensuing action,

Carmela's son seriously wounds Giorgio, beats Ercole about the head, and, with his mother's help, pretty well demoralizes the whole household before he escapes. Carmela, however, is caught and proudly tells all. Later, when the furor dies down, Senter helps her escape; old Giorgio recovers and is "handsomely" pensioned; and Ercole becomes "a magnate among gondoliers."

There are some nice touches in this tale. Miss Senter, for instance, is "chronically annoyed" that she and her brother do not possess the "state entrance" to their palace (the ground floor, or "water-floor," as it is called in Venice, is rented by a dealer in "antiquities"); and Peter Senter thinks that Barbara's knowledge of languages must be "large" because the bills for her instruction in the various tongues have been "large." The suspense in the narrative is nicely maintained, though the denouement seems a bit contrived and melodramatic. From the point of view of a mother's genuine concern for her son's safety, Carmela's part in the story appears reasonable enough, but one wonders if the feats she accomplishes at the age of seventy-four are not a little fantastic (it takes four men to capture and hold her after her son escapes). A mother's sacrifice for her son makes as much sense today as it did in the past, but even in the twentieth century there is a limit to the physical strength and endurance of a woman of seventy-four.

The last piece in this collection actually was the first to appear in a magazine. "In Venice" came out in the *Atlantic* in April, one month prior to the appearance of "The Street of the Hyacinth" in the *Century*. Like "A Christmas Party," "In Venice," as the title indicates, contains a Venetian background; and the characters are, as formerly, Americans in the Old World. The group consists of Mrs. Sophy Marcy, an elderly lady of means; Claudia Marcy, her niece; Rodney Blake, Mrs. Marcy's old friend; Stephen Lenox, a man of taste whose interests in painting have been pursued recently with the help of an inheritance; Elizabeth Lenox, his faithful and loving wife; and Theocritus, Mrs. Lenox's spoiled invalid nephew.

In the story, Claudia, "the personification of healthy life and vigor," falls in love with Lenox, who is not aware of her feelings. Mrs. Lenox, however, is aware of Claudia's passion, but she has perfect faith in her husband. All members of the group (save Mrs. Lenox, who remains behind to care for Theocritus) join together on an "expedition" into the country to secure information about certain of Titian's sketches. While they are gone, Theocritus dies; and the party, to Mrs. Lenox's dismay, returns without Stephen, who, at Claudia's request, has gone even farther into the countryside in the hope of finding the sketches. Claudia immediately assumes the responsibility for Stephen's absence during the boy's funeral and expresses her regret to Elizabeth Lenox, who, in turn, tells Claudia that she understands and that, furthermore, she also knows of Claudia's love for Stephen. The younger woman confesses and offers to leave Venice at once, but Elizabeth persuades her to stay and face up to her situation. A bit later the group disperses: the Lenoxes return to America and the others leave for Baden-Baden, but only Mrs. Lenox knows of Claudia's regard for her husband; and Claudia, with the help of her natural rival, grows through pain and unhappiness to a new measure of maturity.

The materials in this story are hardly unusual ones, but they are handled with care and discrimination. This is no ordinary triangle. Elizabeth's supreme confidence in her husband allows her to be patient and understanding when she becomes aware of Claudia's involvement; and her example, in turn, encourages the younger woman to make the right moral decision. Moreover, Stephen is hardly a part of the triangle since he is never aware of Claudia's interest in him. The approach to this time-worn device is different, and the restraint with which Miss Woolson handles the theme is admirable. This refreshing treatment of the material and some fine character studies make "In Venice," after "The Front Yard" and "The Street of the Hyacinth," one of the best stories in the collection.[29]

Any appraisal of *The Front Yard and Other Italian Stories* should take into account the fact that Miss Woolson apparently did not revise and prepare these pieces for publication in book form as was her usual custom.[30] With this in mind, one may venture to suggest that, with the exception of the three pieces mentioned above (and perhaps "The Pink Villa"), the stories in this volume are not so good as much of James's work in this vein nor, indeed, quite so good as Miss Woolson's own best tales of lake-country or Southern origin. Her technique and style in the Italian stories have improved over that displayed in the earlier short fiction, but her handling of character and use of background material suggests no great advance over the best of her earlier work.

There is, however, something to be said in behalf of this book. A reviewer in the *Critic* summed up its merits in 1895:

> It is a noble legacy that Miss Woolson has left us in these six stories drawn from her heart. They are the product of her life in Italy, but are, nevertheless, more American than many a tale whose scene of action is upon our own soil. In making her home in a strange country, Miss Woolson did not expatriate herself; on the contrary, this alienation seems to have given her a clearer appreciation of the American character, a warmer liking for its nobility, a greater tolerance for its defects. She has an affection even for those idiosyncracies of ours that are sometimes most trying; and there is a kind of loving touch in her treatment of them. It is evident, too, that her studies of Italian life are drawn from the inside, sympathetically; and the contrast between the Americans she introduces, and their environment, brings into striking prominence their peculiarities of character. . . . Nothing in the book . . . is uninteresting, and to those of us who admired Miss Woolson's earlier short stories more than her long novels, and who mourned her untimely death, this volume will be especially welcome [439-40].

One can find little to quarrel with in this judgment. If it is generous in some ways, it is at the same time generally fair in its consideration of Miss Woolson's approach to the stories in this collection. They may add up to something less than a "noble legacy" on the one hand, but they represent, on the other, work that neither James nor Howells need have been ashamed of. Constance Woolson's art, as Quinn has pointed out in another connection, "is a fine art; one returns to her fiction for the sheer joy in well-controlled creation."

IV *Dorothy*

Dorothy and Other Italian Stories (1896)[31] also appeared posthumously, and though the volume may have been planned, along with *The Front Yard,* before Miss Woolson died, she probably did not make the final selection of the pieces to be included. At any rate, the volume, which came out shortly before the second anniversary of her death, contained five items. Among them are "A Florentine Experiment," her first " 'foreign' sketch," and "A Waitress," her last published story.[32]

All of these stories deal with Americans in Europe and, more particularly, in Italy, since each—with the exception of "At the Château of Corinne"—contains an Italian setting. They also develop, in one way or another, some aspect of love as a theme. "A Florentine Experiment" illustrates both of these points very nicely. In the first place, the story is about Americans in Florence, and, in the second place, the situation revolves around the experience of two young Americans, Margaret Stowe and Trafford Morgan, as they "experiment" with love.

Margaret Stowe, the niece but not the heiress of her well-to-do American aunt Miss Harrison, meets Morgan after he has fallen in love with and declared himself to Margaret's best friend, Beatrice Lovell. Unaware at the time that Margaret knows of his feelings for Beatrice, Trafford sees a great deal of her and comes to think that she has fallen in love with him, though Margaret tells him that she has been "experimenting" with him to see if she can forget a former lover. After a separation of a year, the two meet again in Florence, and since Beatrice has married again, Morgan asks Margaret to cooperate with him in an "experiment" to forget his former love. She tacitly consents, but the arrangement is quickly terminated when Morgan proposes marriage on the basis of Margaret's love for him. Later, after another interval, the two are brought together for a third "experiment," this time by Miss Harrison herself. Knowing that the two young people are in truth very much attracted to each other, she contrives to bring them together by telling Morgan that Margaret is to be married. Thinking that he is about to lose Margaret, Morgan confesses his love for her and also admits that his feeling for Beatrice was merely one of fascination. In the Duomo, as a result of Miss Harrison's "Florentine experiment," the two lovers pledge themselves to each other.

Doubtless much of the Florentine background and the discussion of art between Margaret and Morgan are based on Miss Woolson's first visit to Florence in 1880 and on her tours of the museums and galleries with Henry James. Concerning James's friendly attentions, she wrote Samuel Mather on June 8, 1880: "In this connection, I enjoyed very much being with Henry James, who was a delightful companion, and, in addition, very kind to me. . . . He is a very quiet fellow; and very (although in an unobtrusive way) *English.* I put in the correction, because I have seen so many Americans in the last ten years who were 'English' *obtrusively.*"[33]

Kern relates Miss Woolson's friendship with James to "A Florentine Experiment":

> Miss Woolson . . . is transmitting to her readers the information about Italian art and history recently acquired in her studies and in her conversations with Henry James. In fact, the comments of the lovers on painting and on life are probably very similar to those exchanged by Miss Woolson and Henry James in their walking tours of Florence. One detects echoes of James in the cultivated Trafford that are adventitious reminders of the association of the two expatriated writers under circumstances in many ways analogous to the situation of the lovers in the story [118-19].

One cannot help wondering how closely "analogous" the "situation" of Miss Woolson and James was to that of the lovers in the tale. In any event, Miss Woolson's later comment on Morgan's character is suggestive, though I do not think it should be taken as applying directly to James: "I think men like 'Trafford' generally *are* conceited, but that is not the worst of it; the worst is that they are generally, also, so charming (in other ways) that one has to accept the 'conceit' to get the rest! As Margaret did" (Benedict, II, 199n).

"At the Château of Corinne," the second piece in this collection, is set in Switzerland on the shores of Lake Leman in the area of Jacques Necker's old estate and the chateau of Corinne at Coppet; but, like "A Florentine Experiment," its chief characters are Americans and its action involves a series of complications in a love affair. The romance concerns Katharine Winthrop, a wealthy young widow, and John Ford, a cultivated American whose aplomb reminds one of Trafford Morgan's self-assurance.

As the tale begins, Mrs. Winthrop has taken a villa on Lake Leman (The Lake of Geneva) and has as her guests her cousin, Miss Sylvia Pitcher, who is also John Ford's aunt; and H. Walpole, Miss Sylvia's cousin who is referred to by all as "Cousin Walpole." Later two other guests arrive—Ford himself and the poet Lorimer Percival, who becomes a suitor for Mrs. Winthrop's hand. With this cast the little closet drama moves on to the chateau of Corinne, with many references to Madame de Staël and the "distinguished society of Coppet."[34] There, a few days later, Ford finds Katharine Winthrop alone and gives vent to some opinions concerning "literary women" that presumably coincided with Miss Woolson's own personal views. After pointing out that

Madame de Staël was an "inordinate egotist" and that "all her books were talked into existence" on the basis of what she could extract from the conversation of her guests, Ford characterizes the "woman of genius" in general: "And what is the very term but a stigma? No woman is so proclaimed by the great brazen tongue of the Public unless she has thrown away her birthright of womanly seclusion for the miserable mess of pottage called 'fame'" (263).[35] Since Mrs. Winthrop has dabbled a bit in literature herself (she has written and published a little book-length poem), this strikes home. In response to her request for criticism of her work, Ford forthrightly condemns the poem and leaves Coppet under the cloud of his hostess's anger. Several months later he returns from a summer in Scotland to find that she has ridden again to Coppet. Knowing that Percival has married another woman and that much of Mrs. Winthrop's fortune has been lost, Ford follows her to the chateau, confesses his love, and pleads his cause successfully despite his old-fashioned view that women should marry and be dependent upon their husbands.

Kern gives this piece short shrift. Its characters, he points out, "are little more than stock figures in the author's repertory of romance," but Quinn comes a little closer to a fair estimate of the story's value when he remarks that Miss Woolson "puts the case for her own manner brilliantly" in this work. One may question the brilliance with which the case is put before the reader, but there is little room to question the views expressed here concerning the literary amateur and the limitations of certain types of female writers. Miss Woolson has certainly told better stories, but nowhere does she make a more earnest effort to point out the inadequacy of the sentimental approach to literature. John Ford tells Katharine Winthrop that "women do not believe in truth for its own sake; it strikes them as crude." No American writer in the late nineteenth century respected the truth more than Constance Woolson, but one infers from this story and others that she was not always able to overcome the frailties of her sex and that, on occasion, the truth did appear to be too "crude" for literature as she viewed it.[36]

The remaining stories contain Italian backgrounds and deal with some aspect of love as a theme. "Dorothy," the title-piece of this collection, gives Miss Woolson an opportunity to treat unappreciated love in a way that is at least different in circumstance and outcome from the way she handles it in other works of fiction. In this instance, death brings about the denouement.

Dorothy North, stepdaughter of Mrs. Laura North and niece of Mrs. Charlotte Tracy, wealthy Americans who live at Bellosguardo in Florence (an area where Miss Woolson herself lived for several years), marries Alan Mackenzie, a rich fellow countryman whom she does not love. When he dies suddenly of the fever in Rome, she begins to discover too late that she loved him. At first she makes a sincere effort to avoid the consequences of her feelings, but when she fails, she gradually pines away until she dies of a broken heart at nineteen. Aside from the locale, which is summoned up for the reader quite well (the Villa Dorio of the story is actually Miss Woolson's own Villa Castellani), and the introduction into the plot of a song by her friends Francis Boott and John Hay,[37] there is really little to prevent this from being, as Kern has pointed out, "an exceedingly sentimental tale" and "one of the least happy of its author's European stories." Indeed, one might readily suggest that "Dorothy" is exactly the sort of fiction that Miss Woolson opposes in "At the Château of Corinne." Why it was given the place of honor in this volume may not easily be ascertained now, but it seems likely that officials at Harper and Brothers selected one or two of the stories and arranged for the order of inclusion. Though there is some evidence to suggest that "Dorothy" was not unpopular in the 1890's, the story has not worn so well as some of Miss Woolson's other efforts in this vein.

"A Transplanted Boy," though sentimental in spots, is a better piece of work than "Dorothy" and has become one of the favorite stories of Miss Woolson's readers.[38] The situation developed in this tale is not completely original in conception or treatment. Certainly the idea of centering the action around a young American boy who adores his pretty mother is not new—Mrs. Burnett, for instance, had used a similar situation effectively only a few years before in *Little Lord Fauntleroy* (1886). Nor was the idea of showing the influences of "family" and Europe on a young American boy quite a new one—Henry James had done this with Morgan Moreen in "The Pupil" (1891) on a scale and with an artistry that Miss Woolson could hardly hope to emulate. Yet she does have something to offer in "A Transplanted Boy," and she presents it with care as she keeps an omniscient eye trained on the predicament of a thirteen-year-old boy who does not look "to be more than eleven."

Maso (the short form of Thomas in Italian), "a creature all hands and feet, with a big uncertain mouth and an omnipresent awkwardness," has inherited none of his pretty mother's grace and charm; but he possesses qualities of courage and loyalty and self-denial that make up for any lack of outward beauty. When Mrs. Roscoe, Maso's mother, becomes ill and Dr. Prior prescribes a holiday of "at least four months" for her at Aix-les-Bains, Maso sees to it that her mind is made easy with regard to his situation. He also manages later to keep Mrs. Roscoe from knowing that Mr. Waterhouse, the tutor in whose charge Maso has been left, has been called to England. Thus Maso is left to his own devices. Seeking help from an American consul, he fails miserably at first because he knows little about the Declaration of Independence and, later, because he becomes associated in the consul's mind with "the expatriated class." He goes elsewhere but finds that work is hard to come by. His fellow Americans offer little help because he is too Italianate, and the Italians have little need for his services, though he finally gets a job selling cheese.

A few months later his hopes are dashed when he receives a letter from his mother informing him that she is going to Paris (the city of her dreams) for a few weeks just when he thought she was returning to Italy. His misery is compounded about this time by the death of his beloved little terrier, Mr. Tiber, and so it is not strange that in this weakened condition he should contract a malarial fever. Fortunately, he is discovered and cared for tenderly by Roberta Spring, an expatriate from New England and one of his mother's friends, who summons Mrs. Roscoe from Paris. Still thinking of his mother, Maso urges her on her arrival not to get sick again. Aware finally of what her son has done, Mrs. Roscoe prepares to take him home to America at last.

The critics have already pointed out several reasons why "A Transplanted Boy" is an effective story. One has remarked on the skill with which Miss Woolson has been "able to put herself in the place of some one else" and "to look at life through his lens, for the time being."[39] That this "some one else" was a small boy makes this effort of the imagination even more remarkable; one critic points out: "Many a woman who has brought up a family of boys has had less sympathy with them, has understood them less intimately than has Miss Woolson" in this tale. Kern has commented on it from a different point of view:

> The story is notable as an interpretation of the effect of long-continued foreign associations upon an American boy. In appearance, manners, and speech Maso becomes indistinguishable from the Italian boys with whom he associates. Even tourists regard Maso as an indigenous Italian product and are surprised to learn of his American ancestry. Miss Woolson was peculiarly qualified to write of such a phenomenon, as only an American who had lived for years among foreign scenes could realize completely the effect of such an environment upon an impressionable child of antecedents very similar to her own [163].

There are one or two other points that should be made. The omniscient point of view is developed consistently, and the focus on Maso is carefully maintained. The story is unfolded as Maso is confronted by life and as he reacts to it. Mrs. Roscoe's self-centeredness helps to point up both Maso's difficulty and his opportunity, and the contrast between the mother's careless attitude towards her son and the son's unselfish concern for his mother is admirably implicit throughout much of the tale. Moreover, though there is a bit of Victorian sentiment present (especially in the death of Mr. Tiber), Miss Woolson handles it with an authority and skill that properly limit its scope, and yet this restraint lends even more poignancy to the boy's plight. As Maso, according to Quinn, "plays a man's part, without heroics," so Miss Woolson sketches his character without overdoing the sentiment inherent in the situation and without exaggerating the qualities of nobility in his actions. The work is indeed, to cite Quinn again, the revelation of "a power that showed no sign of weakening" despite the fact that the story came out about the time Miss Woolson died. It is, according to some, the "last" story she wrote.

Miss Woolson's last published story, "A Waitress," appeared in *Harper's* in June, 1894, several months after her death in January. From the point of view of its quality as a work of fiction, "A Waitress" belongs more with "Dorothy" than with the other tales in this volume. It certainly is not of the same quality as "A Transplanted Boy" and "A Florentine Experiment."

The action of "A Waitress" can be easily outlined. Modesta, a

Madonna-like Tuscan woman, is the waitress referred to in the title. She is a "regular marvel" of a servant to John Dennison, a wealthy American who has lived in Italy for a number of years. Dennison's guest and fellow countryman, Edward Gray, remarks on Modesta's qualities of sentiment and religion; but Dennison knows that there is more to the Italian woman than meets the eye of any foreigner. Later, when Modesta attacks and tries to kill a naïve Swedish girl with whom Goro, her lover, has been flirting, Gray expresses shock and surpise. But Dennison, knowing Tuscans for what they are, merely arranges to have the Swedish girl sent home and provides for the marriage of Modesta and Goro so that the tranquility and order of his home may not be disturbed.

"The story," as Kern says, "was evidently written to illustrate the fact that only by long association and observation can an American understand and sympathize with those idiosyncrasies of the Latin race which are quite baffling to the newcomer" (164). Such an idea may of course be treated in fiction, but one cannot help feeling that in this piece the characters and the situations have been too carefully devised to fit the thesis Kern has described. Modesta herself never comes alive, and the story therefore fails to materialize. One can only regret that the editors at Harper's did not choose a better piece of work.[40]

What, in the final analysis, may one say about these European stories? Richardson has pointed out that they "have all the originality of [Miss Woolson's] earlier stories, and some of them, such as 'The Front Yard' and 'The Street of the Hyacinth' [both collected in *The Front Yard*], show an increased awareness of technique." A more general estimate was made by a writer in the *Atlantic* two years after Miss Woolson's death:

> Miss Woolson was so much at home in Italy that she could write stories with the scenes laid there and not give one the sense that she was using Italian properties. As in other cases, her interest was in her characters, and a fine perception of delicate shades was kept warm and human by a generous humor. The art of these stories is so good, the breeding so high, that one would fain believe they have a greater enduring power than many more in the fashion of the hour.[41]

From the vantage point of the mid-twentieth century, one might suggest that he is more aware of the "Italian properties" now than he wishes to be and that some of these stories have "endured" better than others. "A Florentine Experiment," "At the Château of Corinne," and "A Transplanted Boy" are, for one reason or another, worthy of our attention today. Such is not the case with "Dorothy" and "A Waitress"; nevertheless, even these tales may be studied with profit as the failures of an artist dedicated to her calling.

CHAPTER 3

The "Evolution of Personal Relations": The Novels

IN MUCH THE SAME WAY that she had related description and background to her composition of sketches and stories, did Miss Woolson relate expository material to her long fiction. As her residences had affected her short pieces, so they also influenced her longer work. Thus her first novel, *Anne* (1882), though written mainly while she was in the South, dealt chiefly with Mackinac, New York, and Cleveland and only incidentally with the South. Her other long works of fiction have Southern settings, but the scene in *Jupiter Lights* (1889) shifts for a time to the lake country and later to Italy.

In practicing the art of the novel, Miss Woolson became interested in the analysis of character and in technique. She considered herself a realist in the sense that she tried to deal with "real life" and sought to probe the minds of her characters in order to examine their motives and relate them honestly to their actions. She acknowledged that she had read George Eliot and Turgenev with profit, but her realism was not similar to that of Balzac or Mark Twain. Her approach to realism and her interest in the psychological novel, on the other hand, were so close to the ideas and practice of James and Howells that in her own day and since she was frequently associated with them in the minds of many, either as peer or follower.

Her novels were not easily written. Each one of them took years of preparation and work. She began to think about writing a novel as early as September, 1874, but she did not actually begin writing until later. In July, 1876, she wrote E. C. Stedman that she was at work on a novel; almost two years later, in May,

1878, she informed him that it was "finished" though not yet "copied." Two and a half more years passed before *Anne* began to appear in *Harper's* in December, 1880.[1] The dates of publication in book form of the other long works of fiction suggest something of the labor each demanded of her: *For the Major* (1883); *East Angels* (1886); *Jupiter Lights* (1889); and *Horace Chase* (1894).

I *Anne*

Anne was serialized in *Harper's* and brought out in book form by the Harper publishing firm shortly after the last installment had appeared in the May, 1882, issue of the magazine.[2] A British reviewer sized up the work by describing it as "holding a place midway between the old American novel of incident and the modern American novel of analysis."[3] The action takes place in locations the author knew at first hand: Mackinac Island, New York City, Pennsylvania, eastern Ohio, and West Virginia. The scene shifts leisurely from place to place, and Miss Woolson carefully and graphically outlines each area. One could almost divide the action of the work by the major changes in locale.

Into this background the characters are introduced. Anne Douglas, from whom the book derives its title, serves as the chief source of unity as the plot moves from the domestic drama of Mackinac to the public drama of the murder trial and its results in Pennsylvania at the end. All the characters, major and minor, are associated in one way or another with Anne, and Miss Woolson makes vivid use of contrast in the employment and development of these characters. Anne's lover, Ward Heathcote, an indolent and sophisticated New Yorker, serves as a nice foil to the innocent, country-bred heroine. His wife, the beautiful socialite Helen Lorrington, Anne's friend and champion during the difficult days with Grandaunt Vanhorn, provides a direct contrast in feminine wiles to the utter guilelessness of Anne. Gregory Dexter, a self-made man and another of Anne's suitors, acts as a contrast to Heathcote. And the use of contrast in characterization applies even in relatively minor figures. William Douglas, Anne's father, represents, for example, the dreamer—"vague, irresolute, imaginative"—as contrasted with the hard-headed practicality and bedrock puritanism of his old friend, Miss Lois Hinsdale. Miss Lois' New England qualities are also contrasted to the easygoing, liberal (but also very practical) qualities of Père Michaux, a cultivated Roman Catholic priest of the Mackinac area.

The plot is fairly complicated, though one may readily follow its convolutions by keeping a steady eye on the movements of the heroine. The action begins on Mackinac Island, Miss Woolson's beloved summer retreat. The characters are gradually introduced and described. Anne's struggles to maintain her father's home are outlined and her chief helpers—Miss Lois and Père Michaux—appear prominently in the action. Her own minister, the absentminded Anglican scholar Dr. James Gaston, makes his contribution and assumes his role as something of a mild contrast to the French priest. William Douglas dies early in the novel, and Anne decides to appeal for help to Miss Katharine Vanhorn, her dead mother's rich aunt in New York. With the proviso that Anne is thereafter to make her own way, Miss Vanhorn grudgingly agrees to support Anne for one year at Madame Moreau's school for young ladies in Manhattan. Anne accepts the condition, but before she can leave Mackinac, her childhood sweetheart, Rast Pronando, proposes to her. Thus she goes to a new world as one already spoken for.

In New York City she meets with success at Madame Moreau's school (Madame herself is kind); and Helen Lorrington, a rich young widow, becomes her friend and puts some effective pressure on Miss Vanhorn to pay more attention to her grandniece. Though Miss Vanhorn is violently upset when she learns of Anne's engagement to young Pronando (by an odd coincidence the old lady had been jilted in her youth by Pronando's father), she takes Anne for the summer vacation to Caryl's, a country place where certain members of New York society congregate. There Anne meets, among others, Ward Heathcote and Gregory Dexter. Helen Lorrington is also there, but is called away for a few days. During her absence Anne falls in love with Heathcote and rejects a proposal from Dexter, despite her grandaunt's efforts to maneuver him into position for this purpose.

When Anne refuses to reconsider her decision regarding Dexter, Miss Vanhorn dismisses her, and she is forced to seek help from her friend Madame Pitre, Madame Moreau's eccentric former associate. With the assistance of Madame Pitre, Anne finds a job as teacher, but on the journey to Ohio where the school is located, they are intercepted by Heathcote, who forthwith proposes to Anne. Having learned that Helen thinks herself betrothed to Ward and remembering her own engagement to Rast, Anne has no choice but to reject the proposal.

Leaving the man she loves, Anne proceeds to her new teaching post and shortly thereafter volunteers as a nurse to tend sick and wounded Union soldiers in the mountains of West Virginia. While performing these new duties, she discovers that Heathcote (now an officer in the Union Army) lies ill of a fever in a near-by hamlet. She goes to him at once, and as he recuperates, he deceives her into thinking that Helen Lorrington has married someone else. Since Pronando has in the meantime married Tita, her self-centered younger sister, Anne now feels free to express openly her feelings for Heathcote. After an exchange of expressions of love, Ward confesses that he has married Helen, and Anne leaves him again.

Returning to the East, Anne manages, with the help of Herr Scheffel, one of her old teachers at Madame Moreau's, to get some music pupils in New York and to catch a few glimpses of the Heathcotes when Ward is home on leave. Dexter, now an important wartime administrative official, appears on the scene to help in various material ways. The stability Dexter introduces into her life is short-lived, and the pattern is broken immediately when Anne sees Heathcote's name on a casualty list in a newspaper. She rushes to console Helen, who later discovers that her husband's name had been placed on the list in error, though she is informed that he had been wounded in the fighting. Helen leaves at once for the front, and on the return journey, in the company of her wounded husband, she is murdered in a small town near the Pennsylvania-Maryland boundary line. Heathcote is immediately suspected, and when he is tried for his wife's murder, the circumstantial evidence against him seems strong, but Anne comes forward to testify concerning motive and her testimony leads to a hung jury. In the period following the trial, Anne and Miss Lois and Père Michaux do some detective work and discover the real killer. Heathcote is released and vindicated in the press. He returns to the army and Anne goes to Mackinac. Two years later, with the war over and peace declared, Heathcote and Anne, in traditional epilogue fashion, are reunited and married on the island.

No summary, of course, can do justice to the vitality and charm of a work that appeared in eighteen issues of a monthly magazine and covered 540 closely printed pages in book form. In this instance, a précis tends to overemphasize the melodramatic qualities in the novel, though it may also suggest some of the problems the novelist has faced. In the case of *Anne*, for example, Miss Woolson did not solve several important problems raised by the length and quality of her materials, as one may infer from a careful reading of the summary. The novel tends to be episodic—Horace E. Scudder pointed out in the *Atlantic* in July, 1882, that it suggested a "series of shorter stories"—and lacks, as Scudder further opined, "a strong controlling, determining purpose, which really moulds circumstance, even when circumstance seems most supreme." Moreover, from the point of view of the twentieth-century reader, Anne's character is too idealized in both conception and development. This is not to say, of course, that in terms of the 1880's Anne does not represent the possibilities of "real life"; certainly her character seems no less "realistic" than, say, that of Marcia Gaylord in Howells' *A Modern Instance* or even, in some respects, of Isabel Archer in James's *Portrait of a Lady,* novels appearing concurrently with *Anne* in the magazines. Still, Anne's self-sacrificing attitude toward her family and her lover and her relations with Helen and Heathcote and Dexter reflect a quality that strikes the modern reader immediately as old-fashioned.

There are, however, other things to be said about Anne's character. She is not characterized sentimentally. Miss Woolson has no desire to milk tears from the reader; rather she would leave him exalted by Anne's noble example of love and self-sacrifice. In this sense at least her purpose belongs more to an "idealistic" rather than to a "realistic" approach to fiction. Anne is also carefully analyzed. Her motives and reactions are elaborately described and discussed, and the reader is given more than ample information from which to draw conclusions concerning her thoughts and actions. It is the "mental problem," as Miss Woolson once phrased it, that intrigues the author. There are times when this fondness for analysis impedes the action of the plot and robs the reader of filling out the outlines of the character for himself, but, more often than not, the analysis leads to an enrichment of characterization that readers accustomed to the refinements of Henry James would be loath to lose.

The other characters in general follow this approach, though there are some sharply focused vignettes among the minor characters: the hard-hearted old Knickerbocker, Miss Vanhorn;

the shrewd and worldly-wise Madame Moreau; the parsimonious but warm-hearted Madame Pitre; the light-hearted, self-centered Rast Pronando; and the generous but opinionated Herr Scheffel, to mention only a few. The number of well-drawn characters is impressive, but several of the major characters have not retained their vitality and authenticity so well as have a number of minor ones. Part of this is due to the fact that Heathcote and Dexter, among the major participants, are chiefly stock figures; part is due to Miss Woolson's limited knowledge of men and their ways.

With regard to matters of setting and style, *Anne* appears dated, but there is much of value inherent in these elements of the work. As a keen observer of nature and of the flora and fauna of the regions in which she lived, Miss Woolson has no difficulty in realizing for the reader the setting she wishes him to visualize and the atmosphere she desires him to feel. One is aware that she describes the various locales in the novel from firsthand knowledge and experience. An early local colorist, she not only treats her scenery and backgrounds with accuracy as regards region but she also gives careful attention to such matters as local custom and speech patterns. In *Anne,* for example, Miss Woolson essays, among others, the French patois of Mackinac, the elegant diction of New York society, a comic German version of English, the Negro dialect of West Virginia, and the speech of the West Virginia mountaineer. All of these she does with an awareness that written dialect must appeal to both eye and ear and that, even when it is written as fluently and gracefully as George W. Cable was writing it in *The Grandissimes* (another novel concurrently serialized with *Anne* in the magazines), it has its limitations. A brief passage of dialogue will illustrate Miss Woolson's reproduction of Negro dialect: " 'Now do be keerful, miss,' urged July, keeping Anne's mule back. 'I'll jes' go and peer roun' a bit. But you stay hyar with Di.' 'Yes, miss,' said Diana. 'We'll go back in de woods a piece, and wait. July'll fin' out all about 'em' " (375).

In certain qualities of technique, Miss Woolson is a creature of her time, though her work reflects a closer kinship to the approach of James or Howells than to that of Twain or Crane. She approaches her story through an omniscient point of view that avoids for the most part interfering with the development of the narrative or with the analysis of character. The comments or asides that reveal the point of view of a nonparticipant in the action as often as not are appropriate to the action and are frequently quite brief. After describing, for example, Madame Moreau's skillful handling of Miss Vanhorn's first visit to Anne at school, the comment is simply: "Ah! skillful old Tante, what a general you would have made!" (154).

Moreover, the point of view does not intrude on the development of character, which is revealed through dialogue and action and analysis. The reader first becomes aware of Miss Lois Hinsdale, as Cowie has pointed out, not through an introduction by the author or by her immediate appearance on the scene but through a discussion of her apropos of other things by William and Anne Douglas. He learns as much about Heathcote from the other characters as he does from the author's analysis of Anne's lover. In the case of the heroine herself, it should be noted that each of these approaches to characterization is employed and that this indirect method is used by both James and Turgenev.

Anne was a popular novel in the 1880's. The public bought it; and even though some critics remarked its failure to fulfill its promise, they usually characterized it as an advance over Miss Woolson's previous fiction. In a letter of November 12, 1882, E. C. Stedman developed this general view in a warmly enthusiastic manner:

> *Of course* I read 'Anne' seriatim. . . . All in all, I considered it a beautiful work—an epochal stage in your career as a creative writer. And I will say at once that I agree with those critics who think the original, faultless, creative manner and standard of the first half of the novel in certain respects superior to the remainder. It seemed as if you threw a sop to Cerberus, or adopted a mistaken form of continuance, in relying somewhat upon realistic plot and counterplot for the disposition of your characters. Your true self, your highest and most creative standard, are found in the early portraitures; in the ideal and growth of your large-moulded heroine. But as a first novel, 'Anne' is a noble effort, confirming me in my early belief that you can and will produce masterpieces, and become our foremost writer of imaginative prose [Stedman and Gould, II, 347-48].

Stedman's view of *Anne* has largely been forgotten today and the novel is seldom read, but it is an interesting work of fiction despite its obvious faults. Assuredly, Anne herself seems too noble and self-sacrificing for modern tastes; the book is by its very nature too episodic; and the last part which deals with the murder of Helen Lorrington, the trial of Heathcote, and the subsequent detection of the real murderer is for readers of Agatha Christie and Ellery Queen both too melodramatic and too poorly elaborated. Nevertheless *Anne* offers more than this criticism suggests. The characters, though dated, are believable, given their time and place and atmosphere; and they reflect, in the main, their author's solid knowledge of human nature in a variety of settings and conditions. The story, though it is episodic throughout and melodramatic near the end, achieves an integrity through the consistency and vitality of its central character, too magnanimous though she may be. In some matters of style and technique the work also appears to belong to another era, but Miss Woolson tells her tale with an enviable grace and charm and with a naïveté that is positively refreshing in this sophisticated day and age. All in all, *Anne* is not a satisfactory work of art, but it has an ingenuous quality which criticism cannot touch and which Miss Woolson's better novels do not possess.

II *For the Major*

In the creation of a fictional world that has a validity of its own and is inhabited by characters whose motives and actions contribute rightfully to the credibility of this world of the imagination, Miss Woolson has produced in *For the Major* (1883) her best long work of fiction.[4] Described by its author as a "novelette," *For the Major* is nevertheless long enough and well developed enough to be considered with Miss Woolson's more lengthy fiction.

The scene is set in Far Edgerley, a village in the mountains of western North Carolina, and more particularly at the "Farms," the home of the Carrolls, the town's first family. The action begins with the return of Sara Carroll after a long sojourn in Connecticut with a wealthy uncle. She is greeted by her stepmother, Madam Carroll, and informed that her father, Major Scarborough Carroll, cannot be disturbed. From this moment on she gradually discovers that her father's mental powers are declining and that Madam Carroll is carefully protecting both him and the village from the knowledge of this fact. Shocked and disturbed, Sara joins forces with her stepmother in this good cause, and the Major is put on exhibit for the villagers only at carefully selected occasions: receptions at the "Farms" and Sunday worship at St. John's Episcopal Church. Even Frederick Owen, the personable young rector, is not aware of Major Carroll's infirmity.

Into this delicate situation Louis Dupont, a total stranger, thrusts himself, seemingly with little effort despite Far Edgerley's well-known reputation for reserve. Dupont is something of an exotic, a musician from the "West India Islands," and Owen finds it difficult to believe that he has been accepted so quickly and so warmly by the ladies (especially by Sara Carroll) at the "Farms." To Owen's relief, however, Dupont leaves as suddenly as he had come; but, within a few days, he returns quite ill. In a feverish condition, he is cared for by half the population of the town, including the Carroll ladies. Despite these ministrations, Dupont dies and Owen (but not the village) learns that he had been Madam Carroll's son by an earlier husband; and then the story of her life previous to her marriage to the Major is told.

She had been first married to a man whose shameful conduct had forced him to run for his life. Taking their only son with him, he made his escape when his pursuers thought him drowned in a river. The young wife also thought her spouse dead and that she was therefore free to marry when, ten years later, Major Carroll proposed to her. Accepting him gratefully, she did not tell the Major about her past since he seemed to take joy in her youthful freshness. For all the years of her second marriage Madam Carroll used every feminine device to maintain the fiction of her ageless beauty. Dupont's arrival on the scene had put her in a quandary, but Sara had agreed to help; and the situation was managed, though Owen could not help misunderstanding some of the maneuvers involved. With Dupont's death and Major Carroll's decline to complete senility, Madam Carroll's disguise is discarded, and she emerges as the old and tired woman she really is. Sara and Owen, responding to this woman's courage and devotion and sacrifice, arrange for another marriage ceremony between the master and the mistress of the "Farms."

As one may observe from the foregoing summary of the plot, the central situation involves the role Madam Carroll plays before her husband and the village. In protecting him and the people of the community she displays a high-minded selflessness that exalts her and transcends the petty deceptions to which she has resorted. Henry James discusses this point in his essay on Miss Woolson:

> Miss Woolson's women in general are capable of these refinements of devotion and exaltations of conscience, and she has a singular talent for making our sympathies go with them. The conception of Madam Carroll is highly ingenious and original, and the small stippled portrait has a real fascination. It is the first time that a woman has been represented as painting her face, dyeing her hair, and 'dressing young,' out of tenderness for another: the effort usually has its source in tenderness for herself. But Miss Woolson has done nothing of a neater execution than this fanciful figure of the little ringleted, white-frocked, falsely juvenile lady, who has the toilet-table of an actress and the conscience of a Puritan [183].

Thus Madam Carroll possesses the dominant characteristic one finds in Anne before her and in Margaret Harold after her. All three of these heroines live by principle and subordinate themselves to their duty as they conceive of it. Of these, Madam Carroll's sacrifice may seem more credible to some, for she works to protect her husband and his position in the community, whereas Anne and Margaret sacrifice their love for moral principle. At any rate, it is clear that Madam Carroll represents one of Miss Woolson's best efforts to draw a high-minded female character whose sacrifice ennobles not only her own life but that of others as well.

The other characters in *For the Major* are done with the author's usual care: Major Carroll, the declining old aristocrat who somehow retains his dignity despite his approaching senility; Sara, the beautiful and devoted daughter who responds immediately to the needs of both her father and stepmother. Frederick Owen, the eligible young rector whose love for Sara puts him in a very delicate position at times; Senator Ashley, a gentleman of the old school whose delightfully dated conversation provides some of the work's nicest touches of humor; and the various townspeople who manifest on occasion the universal qualities associated with village folk (the ladies of the St. John's choir, for example, are a case in point).

In *For the Major*, as a matter of fact, Miss Woolson presents some of her most delightful minor characters, many of whom are introduced chiefly to illustrate some aspect of life in Far Edgerley. The gossipy Mrs. Greer, for instance, represents the social side of life in the town, and her efforts to sound out Mr. Owen on the matter of a "Whist Club" ("there were persons in the congregation who considered whist-playing a test of the best churchmanship") are among the best examples of humor in the book. Miss Woolson is too good an artist to allow a character of Mrs. Greer's quality to leave the stage too soon, for one who thinks whist "a climate by itself—a climate of geniality" must have other contributions to make in a small community. And, right away, one finds that Mrs. Greer also serves, unbeknownst to herself, as a disseminator of news Madam Carroll wishes to spread around the village. The rest is too beautifully indicative of Miss Woolson's art at its best to be paraphrased:

> Mrs. Greer had collected a large assortment of phrases from the overflow of the Farms. These she treasured, and dealt out one by one; her conversation was richly adorned with them. She had excellent opportunities for collecting, as Madam Carroll had long been in the habit of telling her any little item which she wished to have put in circulation through the village in a certain guise. She always knew that her exact phrase would be repeated, but not as hers; it would be repeated as if it were original with the lady who spoke it. This was precisely what Madam Carroll intended. To have said herself, for instance, that the new chintz curtains of her drawing-room combined delicacy and durability, and a bower-like brightness was too apparent; but for Mrs. Greer to say it (in every house on Edgerley Street) was perfectly proper, and accomplished the same result. The whole town remarked upon the delicacy and the durability and the bower-like brightness; and the curtains, which she had made and put up herself at small expense, took their place among the many other peculiarly admirable things possessed by the Farms [180].

What could be more universal or more charmingly expressed than this!

If the characters in *For the Major* are carefully realized, so also is the setting:

> Edgerley the first lay on the eastern flank of Chillawassee Mountain; Edgerley the second six hundred feet above. The first Edgerley, being nearer the high civilization of the state capital,

> claimed the name, and held it; while the second Edgerley was obliged to content itself with an added 'far.' Far Edgerley did not object to its adjective so long as it was not considered as applying especially to the distance between it and the lower town. It was 'far,' if you pleased—far from cities, far from traffic, from Babylon, from Zanzibar, from the Pole—but it was not 'far' from Edgerley. Rather was Edgerley far from it, and—long may she keep so! [1].

Though Miss Woolson wrote Stedman on April 30, 1883, that *For the Major* was a "little genre picture of village life, with strong local color," she apparently did not believe she should confine herself to a local-color approach in the treatment of her setting. Henry James, for example, gathered "vaguely" that the scene was set in "the south," though he recognized Miss Woolson's "high sense of the picturesque" and her fondness for "a social atmosphere" (185). Far Edgerley is also characterized by its people in a manner reminiscent of Jane Austen. The reader's view of the town takes on dimensions as he observes the people's distrust of the "commercial" Edgerley; as he becomes aware of their hospitality and concern for others, even a stranger such as Louis Dupont; and as he comes to know their customs and manners and attitudes.

> . . . there was no longer much curiosity about Miss Carroll. It was feared that she was 'cold'; and it was known that she was 'silent'; she had almost no 'conversation.' Now, Far Edgerley prided itself upon its conversation. It never spoke of its domestic affairs in company; light topics of elegant nature were then in order. Mrs. Greer, for instance, had Horace Walpole's letters—which never failed. Other ladies preferred the cultivation of flowers, garden rock-work, and their bees (they allowed themselves to go as far as bees, because honey, though of course edible, was so delicate). Mrs. Rendlesham, who was historical, had made quite a study of the characteristics of Archbishop Laud. And the Misses Farren were greatly interested in Egyptian ceramics. Senator Ashley, among many subjects, had also his favorite; he not infrequently turned his talent for talking loose upon the Crimean War. This was felt to be rather a modern topic. But the junior warden was, on the whole, the most modern man they had. Too modern, some persons thought [77].

In regard to style and technique, *For the Major* is certainly one of Miss Woolson's most impressive performances. The omniscient point of view is controlled successfully and concentrated on Madam Carroll, but since the narration is developed by an omniscient entity, the totality of characters and village can easily be encompassed. This is accomplished with a maximum of efficiency and a minimum of commentary. The story line is seldom obstructed by excessive analysis of characters as it sometimes is in *Anne* or *East Angels,* and the central situation is handled with considerable economy, restraint, and skill. The concluding scenes are done in a rather modern manner. The author refuses to spell out Madam Carroll's appeal to Owen for help; the reader is left to surmise that she has asked him to marry her again to the Major and that Owen has accepted the larger principle, for at the end he reads the ceremony and the elderly couple repeats the sacred vows. That Miss Woolson handles the whole complicated situation without sentimentality and makes things right in the end without marring the work by imposing a happy ending on it is a real tribute to her integrity as a storyteller of the 1880's.

For the Major was favorably reviewed, in the main, by the chief monthly magazines in 1883. Writers of reviews in *Harper's* in July and in the *Century* in December were enthusiastic in their praise. The first of these, for example, found the novelette a "revelation" of the "increased range" of Miss Woolson's "powers" and the "portrait" of Madam Carroll "one of the most original and most perfect conceptions in modern literature." Reviewers in the *Atlantic* in July and in *Lippincott's* in August were somewhat less enthusiastic, but despite their objections to certain aspects of the work, the former admitted that it was "a very ingenious" and "skillfully managed" story and the latter thought it "rare, delicate, and exquisitely told." Miss Woolson considered it the "best piece of work" she had done, or so she wrote Hamilton W. Mabie on June 18, 1883. In April she had informed Stedman that *For the Major* was "a better piece of work, artistically viewed, than 'Anne'—though its motif will not, I suppose, attract the 'average reader' as that of 'Anne' did."

More recently, *For the Major* has been discussed favorably by Quinn in *American Fiction,* Cowie in *The Rise of the American Novel,* and by Hubbell in *The South in American Literature.* The warmest recent notice of the book appeared in the *Saturday Review of Literature* for October 12, 1929. In that issue was published a long letter from John Hervey of Chicago, in which he commented on the fiction of the 1920's (especially the work of Ellen Glasgow) by comparing it with that of an earlier day. He selected Miss Woolson as an artist of the 1880's and singled out *For the Major* as "one of the little masterpieces of American fiction."

> What makes 'For the Major' live, what gives it its enduring charm, is its perfect sincerity and exquisite sympathy. It is written with a quiet humour that abounds in touches worthy of Jane Austen, with an extraordinary insight and clairvoyance, a lightness of touch that is unfailing. Far Edgerley literally swarms with 'characters' which are brought before us with firm, fine strokes of assured art, but not once, from beginning to end, is there a jeer, a sneer, or a gibe in their depiction. They were created in love and to subject them to such an indignity would have been impossible to their creator [268].

To this, one can only add what Quinn has already said about the novelette: It "reminds one of an etching in which one central figure stands out in exquisite proportions against a background whose very limitations present that figure to perfection. . ." (338).

III *East Angels*

Second only to *Anne* in popularity,[5] *East Angels* (1886) was also well received by the critics. Howells, writing in the "Editor's Study" in *Harper's* in August, 1886, found it difficult to "believe in" Evert Winthrop and Margaret Harold, the lovers whose situation lies at the heart of the work, but he commended the book for "the respect for probability, the fidelity to conditions, human and social, which can alone justify the reading or writing of novels." James, on the other hand, in his essay finds Mrs. Harold a bit "exalted" but at the same time "thoroughly sound." More recently, several critics—Quinn, Cowie, and Wagenknecht—have favorably remarked on Miss Woolson's "finest and most ambitious novel," as Wagenknecht has characterized it.[6] A modern reader is likely to see the justice in all these views, though he may tend to agree with Howells' opinion of the lovers. Despite this possibility, the reader can hardly fail to be impressed by the overall quality of this work of fiction.

The action takes place in a small village in Florida, where, as Cowie points out, the "mise-en-scène is firmly established in all its opulence and fascination." The most important characters are chiefly Northerners who have come south seeking sunshine and rest. There are a number of characters from the South, but, with one exception, they are not central to the development of the action.

In the beginning Evert Winthrop, a wealthy young New York businessman and a descendant of New England pioneers, comes to Florida to relax and to find a suitable resting place for his aunt, Mrs. Rutherford, who is rich enough and selfish enough to enjoy being a "professional invalid," to borrow Quinn's phrase. In Florida, Winthrop meets the Thornes, mother and daughter. Mrs. Thorne, a native of New Hampshire who had married in the South and apparently remained loyal during the "late unpleasantness," is the mistress of "East Angels," an old Spanish home from which the book takes its title; and Edgarda (Garda) Thorne, her young and beautiful daughter whose character reflects in fascinating ways the mixed blood lines of her ancestors from Old England, New England, and Spain, is a brilliant study in self-centeredness and naïve caprice. In order to help the Thornes conquer their genteel poverty, Winthrop agrees to buy "East Angels."

Shortly thereafter, Mrs. Rutherford and her niece-in-law, Mrs. Margaret Harold, who possesses a "quiet reserved sort of beauty," arrive on the scene. Mrs. Harold is the estranged wife of Lansing Harold, Mrs. Rutherford's favorite nephew, and both aunt and Winthrop think that Margaret is responsible for the failure of her marriage. The newcomers are introduced by Winthrop to the local gentry: the Thornes; the Moores—the local Episcopal minister and his delicate invalid wife; the Kirbys—the town physician, an authority on Southern customs and manners, and his aging but discerning mother; Mrs. Carew, a fluttery Southern widow and former school chum of Mrs. Rutherford's in New York, whose penchant for inane allusion reflects a certain lightness in the head which somehow seems not to have affected a corresponding warmness of the heart; Manuel Ruiz, the scion of a neighboring plantation family and a suitor for Garda's hand; and Adolfo Torres, a Cuban who speaks no English until near the end of the novel and who adores Garda silently, persistently, and patiently.

As time passes, Mrs. Thorne's health declines, and when she knows that she is going to die, "the little starved yet ardent daughter of the Puritans" (to quote James) in a passionate outburst of pent-up feeling roundly denounces the place and the region where she has lived so long and proudly reasserts her allegiance to New England in all things. Then, after extracting a promise from Winthrop and Margaret to watch over Garda, Mrs. Thorne finally leaves forever "the idle, unrealizing, contented life of this tiresome, idle coast."

The new guardians take their duty seriously and perform their tasks so well that Winthrop proposes to Garda after unavoidably spending a night on the pine barrens with her and without a chaperone; and Margaret Harold encourages both parties to see that the engagement is to their mutual advantage. But Garda falls in love with Lucian Spenser, a younger engineer and distant relative of the Reverend Moore. Spenser's lighthearted and irresponsible nature appeals mightily to her own egoistic and capricious self, and she breaks the engagement with Winthrop, who learns from his experience that it is Margaret whom he really loves. The Garda–Winthrop affair not only has something in common with the Imogene Graham–Theodore Colville relationship in Howells' *Indian Summer* (1886) but it also prepares Miss Woolson's reader in many ways for the central situation in her last novel, *Horace Chase* (1894), the relationship between Ruth Franklin and Chase himself.[7]

Mrs. Harold, however, is in no position to respond to Evert's expressions of affection, for her long-absent husband returns, and she goes to him when he writes her to come, despite the fact that he has treated her miserably by running off to Europe to carry on an affair with a woman of rank. Winthrop opposes Margaret's decision to return to Harold, and his judgment is vindicated when Lanse fails to live up to his marriage again and returns to his affair in Paris. Margaret continues to refuse Winthrop's love, though she has to admit that she loves him in return; and, in the end, when Harold comes back to her a sick and broken man, she takes him in and accepts her lot with stoical fortitude and self-denial.

In the meantime, Garda has married and later buried Spenser and even toyed with the idea of setting her cap for Winthrop again until she learns the true nature of Margaret's feeling for him. After a "pretty widowhood," as James calls it, she finally gives her hand to Torres, who has at last learned to speak English for himself. Thus *East Angels* comes to an end with the lofty example on the one hand of Margaret's renunciation of the one love of her life, contrasted on the other with the silly spectacle of Garda's marriage to a man for whom she has little respect.

A critical consideration of *East Angels* might well begin with Henry James, and since Miss Woolson devotes a great deal of her talent as a novelist to the development of character and to character analysis, one might expect her friendly contemporary to have something of pith and moment to say about her characters. Certainly the creator of Isabel Archer might be expected to understand and appreciate Margaret Harold's predicament.

> In 'East Angels' the sacrifice . . . is the great sacrifice of Margaret Harold, who immolates herself—there is no other word—deliberately, completely, and repeatedly, to a husband whose behaviour may as distinctly be held to have absolved her. The problem was a very interesting one, and worthy to challenge a superior talent—that of making real and natural a transcendent, exceptional act representing a case in which the sense of duty is raised to exaltation. What makes Margaret Harold's behaviour exceptional and transcendent is that, in order to render the barrier between herself and the man who loves her, and whom she loves, absolutely insurmountable, she does her best to bring about his marriage, endeavours to put another woman into the frame of mind to respond to him in the event . . . of his attempting to console himself for a bitter failure. The care, the ingenuity, the precautions the author has exhibited, to make us accept Mrs. Harold in her integrity, are perceptible on every page, and they leave us finally no alternative but to accept her; she remains exalted, but she remains at the same time thoroughly sound. For it is not a simple question of cleverness of detail, but a question of the larger sort of imagination, and Margaret Harold would have halted considerably if her creator had not taken the supreme precaution of all, and conceived her from the germ as capable of a certain heroism—of clinging at the cost of a grave personal loss to an idea which she believes to be a high one, and taking such a fancy to it that she endeavours to paint it, by a refinement of magnanimity, with still richer hues. She is a picture, not of a woman indulging in a great spasmodic flight or moral *tour de force,* but of a nature bent upon looking at life from a high point of view, an attitude in which there is nothing abnormal, and which the author illustrates, as it were, by a test case. She has drawn Margaret with so close and firm and living a line that she seems to put us in the quandary, if we repudiate her, of denying that a woman *may* look at life from a high point of view.

> She seems to say to us: 'Are there distinguished natures, or are there not? Very well, if there are, that's what they can do—they can try and provide for the happiness of others (when they adore them) even to their own injury.' And we feel that we wish to be the first to agree that there *are* distinguished natures [189-90].

James has more to say, but his analysis of Margaret Harold describes her share in the central situation of the book. Readers will have to make up their minds about her sacrifice—the renunciation of Evert Winthrop's love and the acceptance of her "duty" to Lansing Harold. This action may appear old-fashioned to modern readers to whom divorce is as familiar as the media of mass communication can make it; indeed, Howells long ago remarked on this point. But James has put the problem quite well in his discussion: if one rejects Margaret as being too quixotic and too high-minded, one runs the risk of maintaining a somewhat narrow view of the female in literature or in life—a view, one may add, that denies at its peril the generous impulses of feminine nature. Some readers of the present age doubtless will find Margaret's motivation and action strange and even improbable, but others will judge her on her own terms and conclude that she stands for something that is older and more universal in the canon of man's admirable qualities than many so-called virtues of either the Victorian Age or the Atomic Age: genuine selflessness.

The next question, then, is whether or not Margaret Harold is a believable character on her own terms. Here again one may appeal to James for help. Her character is certainly consistent; "from the germ," as he points out, it has been developed as being of a certain nature. But is she "too good"? That, in the final analysis, is really beside the point, for if her character is consistently and carefully developed and related to both humanity and reality in a psychologically sound way, one can accept it or reject it on the basis of personal opinion or taste, but he cannot so readily attack its validity. Margaret's decision (and her reasons for it) must appear a bit peculiar to many living in America now, but this is more a reflection on the present than a commendation of the 1880's. The treatment of magnanimity and self-sacrifice is valid for any day, even though these virtues frequently tend to be underrated or viewed as quixotic in a brave new world where the ego is king and a constant battle is waged to win man's mind and belly but seldom his immortal soul. At any rate, Margaret's character is of a piece and, as James says, "thoroughly sound."[8]

Of the other characters, several are among the best that Miss Woolson ever created. Garda Thorne, for example, is, as James remarks, "the next best thing in the book to Margaret"; to Howells, she was the "triumph of the book." In her insatiable desire for happiness she reminds one of a certain universal craving among those who have been shielded from life and never taught any responsibility to it. Mrs. Thorne, Mrs. Rutherford, Mrs. Carew, and Dr. Kirby, all minor characters, are sketched with assurance from firsthand experience and with an exquisite awareness of both virtue and foible in each personality. The characterization of Evert Winthrop, on the other hand, is disappointing. Winthrop serves, in some ways, as a sort of preliminary sketch for Horace Chase, but the circumstances of the novel so separate him from the sources of his strength as a successful businessman that he appears more the social lion than the economic bear. He loses thereby (as does Christopher Newman in James's *The American,* 1877) some of the color and vitality associated with the thriving entrepreneur in fiction or life who made his way in the hurly-burly of the American marketplace in the Gilded Age. On the whole, however, the characters and the author's careful analyses of them are among the novel's chief assets. As Howells wrote in the "Editor's Study" in 1886, "they are for the most part, in mood and motive, like people one meets. The least important figure among them is sketched with a feeling for character which leaves it distinct and memorable."

With regard to setting and style and technique, *East Angels* reflects something of an advance over *Anne.* The Florida setting is vividly realized, and the action is confined to this carefully sketched area. As a result, the characters, according to Quinn, "gain each in his own way in vividness from their contrast or association with the rich languor of the Florida landscape" (338). At the same time she has focused her attention on one locale in *East Angels,* Miss Woolson has become more flexible in regard to point of view. In *Anne,* for example, the point of view is omniscient, but the reader is aware that the focus of interest is on Anne herself. The point of view in *East Angels* is still omniscient, but the center of interest shifts on occasion from Garda to Margaret to Winthrop; consequently, the reader becomes aware of a complexity and variety in the novel that may be marked down as evidence of an increasing mastery over this aspect of technique. Certainly, the shift in the angle of vision from which the material is viewed makes possible a richness of comparison and contrast that a more concentrated point of view must forgo.

A word about humor in *East Angels*. Miss Woolson's humor has already been remarked on both as it is expressed in her fiction and in her letters, but a delightful incident in the work at hand provides an apt illustration not only of her use of humor but also of her method of characterizing minor actors in her drama. Towards the middle of the work, Adolfo Torres, Garda's stolid admirer, decides that he must formally make his honorable intentions known to Dr. Kirby, Garda's legal guardian. Torres, of course, can speak no English at the time, and the good doctor can speak no Spanish. This language barrier, however, does not prevent the young Cuban from paying Kirby a formal visit. Torres gravely broaches the subject of his interest in Miss Thorne; Kirby, a Southern gentleman of the old school, politely counters with a discussion of the orange crop for the year. Torres hopes that the guardian will have no objection to his suit; Kirby in turn discourses on several varieties of oranges. Thus the discussion continues until the doctor runs out of "orange" talk and fills out his part of the conversation with two hundred lines from "one of his favorite poems," "The Rape of the Lock." Torres listens to the poem "without change of expression," and when the doctor finishes, he gallantly brings up his proposal again. Finally, Kirby "with a sudden inspiration" offers the Cuban a dictionary, but the suitor is offended and refuses to make a "school exercise" of his suit. Kirby then takes up the dictionary and gradually discovers what Torres is about. Enraged at the thought that Torres seeks an "alliance" when he is "two years under age" and has "nothing in the world to offer a wife" except his "impudence," Kirby adjures him to "go home and play with [his] top!" Torres, of course, does not understand a word of these one-sided remarks. "But he could comprehend the Doctor's opening the door for him; and, with respect unbroken, he formally took leave." Defeated for the moment without knowing why, Torres, ironically enough, wins Garda at last when she has no other suitors to turn to.

In the final analysis, *East Angels* is a good novel. It is rather long, but Miss Woolson is not interested in a fast-paced, simple narrative. She is concerned with character development and analysis, matters that inevitably slow down the pace of fiction. The reader is rewarded for his patience by excellent character studies and vignettes. Readers of the present day who have become accustomed to long works of fiction in the tradition of Thomas Wolfe need not hesitate to tackle *East Angels.* With its carefully sketched Florida background, its varied dramatis personae, its humor and understanding, and its charming re-creation of a world that once was and is no more, the novel is well worth reading today. As Henry James once remarked, "*East Angels* is a performance which does Miss Woolson the highest honour," and, he continued, "if her talent is capable, in another novel, of making an advance equal to that represented by this work in relation to its predecessors, she will have made a substantial contribution to our new literature of fiction" (186). That she was not able to make such an "advance" in her next book should not mar in any way the contribution she made in this one. *East Angels* represents Constance Fenimore Woolson at her very best.

IV *Jupiter Lights*

Miss Woolson once wrote Samuel Mather that *Jupiter Lights* (1889) was "different" from her other novels because it was "shorter, & full of action, with almost no description."[9] Despite this opinion, one notes that the novel is not unlike *Anne* in its episodic character and in its shifts of scene—the action in *Jupiter Lights* begins in the coastal area of Georgia, continues in the lake country, and concludes in Italy. The author seems chiefly interested in the Southern character and environment, as Kern has pointed out in his study (90-91), though she had been living in Europe for a decade when the work appeared in book form. *Jupiter Lights,* moreover, is more melodramatic than its predecessors, and Miss Woolson's examination of the psychological quirks of her characters doubtless provided her publisher with sufficient reason to characterize the novel as her "strongest" work to date.

The story, as is the case with much of Miss Woolson's fiction, is a study in dramatic contrast, and the themes of duty and renunciation are sounded again. Eve Bruce and Cicely Morrison may profitably be compared with Anne Douglas and Helen

Lorrington in *Anne,* with Madam Carroll and Sara Carroll in *For the Major,* and with Margaret Harold and Garda Thorne in *East Angels.* Eve Bruce, for example, represents the high-minded, self-reliant heroine who is willing, like Anne and Margaret before her, to give up the man she loves because she feels that this is her duty; Cicely Morrison, on the other hand, is a self-centered, self-indulgent, pliant female who reminds one of Garda Thorne and Ruth Franklin Chase, a perfect foil to the Eve Bruces of Miss Woolson's fictional world.

The action begins with the arrival of Eve Bruce at "Romney," the home off the Georgia coast (Kern conjectures that the author had Sapelo Island in mind) of Cicely Abercrombie Bruce Morrison, the former wife of Eve's dead brother Jack and the mother of his only child and namesake. After Jack Bruce's death, Cicely married Ferdie Morrison, the scion of a Maryland family and a charming dipsomaniac. Eve is unaware of this union until she arrives at "Romney" for a visit with her nephew and sister-in-law and Cicely's family, the Abercrombies—Sabrina, her old maid aunt, and the elderly Judge, her grandfather. Eve determines to persuade Cicely and Ferdie to give up little Jack so that she may rear him herself. This plan appears doomed when Eve shoots and wounds Morrison, who, in a drunken fit, seeks to kill his wife and stepchild.

Thinking Morrison dead, Eve flees north with Cicely, little Jack, and Judge Abercrombie, who joins them in Charleston. The group then proceeds to Port aux Pins on Lake Superior (Potterpins, as the natives call it), the home of Paul Tennant, Ferdie's half-brother. There Eve and Cicely seek help from Tennant and "disport" themselves for a time. A false report comes from "Romney" that Morrison has been shot by Negroes, and after some time has passed, the news of his death is received by Cicely, whose response is a violent attack of "brain-fever."

Eve, in the meantime, has fallen in love with Paul, but she has been unwilling to divulge this to him, for she thinks that she has killed his brother. Paul at length returns Eve's love, but she refuses him without telling him the real reason for her decision. To make matters more complicated, Christopher Hollis, Paul's friend and a practical, thoughtful Yankee, falls in love with Eve but does not tell her, for he is aware of her feeling for Tennant. When Cicely recovers from her illness, she accuses Eve of killing Ferdie and decides to return to "Romney." Eve nevertheless accompanies her on the journey, and Paul follows them, even though Eve has finally told him that she killed Morrison.

Despite his fondness for Ferdie, Tennant cannot hate Eve. On the contrary, he continues to urge her to marry him; but since she feels that he will later come to hate her for the deed, she declines his proposal again and runs away. In hot pursuit of the maiden, Paul meets in Charleston Dr. Edward Knox, the physician who had attended Morrison in his illness, and discovers that his brother had died from a series of drunken sprees. Knowing at last that his beloved is innocent of Ferdie's death, Paul follows Eve to Italy, where he finds her contemplating offering her services to a "charitable institution." (She is still unaware of the circumstances concerning Morrison's death.) When the authorities exhibit no interest in letting him see Eve and he learns that she has taken no "vows," Paul forces his way into the fourteenth-century villa that houses the order and takes Eve "in his arms." Thus the novel ends on a happy but somewhat melodramatic note.

Such a bare outline as this hardly gives one an adequate idea of the quality of *Jupiter Lights.* There are so many deft little touches in regard to scene, minor characters, and insights into human nature that one may perhaps overlook a bit of melodrama or an erratic shifting of the book's center of interest. One thinks, for example, of the Fourth of July festivities at Port aux Pins which Miss Woolson admitted in a letter to Samuel Mather were "exactly like those we used to have in Cleveland before you were born" (quoted in Richardson, 31). The order of the "procession" on that grand occasion as reported in the Port aux Pins *Eagle* is worthy of quotation in its entirety:

The Marshal of the Day.

The Goddess of Liberty. (Parthenia Drone.)

The Clergy. (In carriages.)

Fire-Engine E. P. Snow

The Major and Common Council. (In carriages.)

Hook and Ladder No. 1.

The Immortal Colonies. (Thirteen little girls in a wagon, singing the 'Red, White, and Blue.')

Fire-Engine Leander Braddock.

> The Carnival of Venice. (This was a tableau. It represented the facade of a Venetian palace, skilfully constructed upon the model of the Parthenon, with Wolf Roth in an Indian canoe below, playing upon his guitar. Wolf was attired, as a Venetian, in a turban, a spangled jacket, high cavalry boots with spurs, and powdered hair; Idora Drone looked down upon him from a Venetian balcony; she represented a Muse.)
>
> Reader of the Declaration Independence, and
> Orator of the Day. (In carriages.)
>
> The Survivors of the War. (On foot with banners.)
>
> Model of Monument to Our Fallen Heroes.
>
> The Band. (Playing 'The Sweet By-and-By.')
>
> Widows of Our Fallen Heroes. (In carriages.)
>
> Fire-Engine Senator M. P. Hagen.
>
> The Arts and Sciences. (Represented by the portable printing-press of the Port aux Pins *Eagle*; wagons from the mines loaded with iron ore; and the drays, coal-carts, and milk-wagons in a procession, adorned with streamers of pink tarlatan) [201-2].

Nor has Miss Woolson forgotten other standard features and the color of the occasion: the cannon "salute," the local militia, the white dresses of the ladies, the "refreshments" (peanuts and lemon candy), the oratory, and the reading of the Declaration to the cheers and hurrahs of a crowd that swayed in turn to the familiar phrases of the document and to the oratorical flourishes of the reader until the final reference to "our lives, our forrchuns, and our sacrred *honor*" brought forth a "roar" of approval. Those who have read nineteenth-century American newspapers will recognize at once that Miss Woolson knew the small-town Fourth of July celebration at first hand.

Jupiter Lights is also blessed with some of Miss Woolson's usual skill in the treatment of minor characters. Judge Abercrombie, a Southern gentleman of the old school, is neatly characterized. A descendant of one of the "signers" of the Declaration and an admirer of the ante-bellum South, he loves his native land. "To him, this Southern coast was fair as Paradise; he welcomed the dark hue of the Southern trees, he welcomed the neglected fields, he even welcomed the broken-down old houses here and there. . . . 'God bless my country!' was the old man's fervent thought. But his 'country' was limited; it was the territory which lies between the St. Mary's River and the Savannah" (306).

There are also, among a number of other sketches in a gallery of Southern characters, brief vignettes of two sisters, the Misses Leontine and Polly Wingfield ("the girls," as they are known to their friends, are merely fifty-two and forty-two, respectively) to whom the Judge and his ladies (Cicely and Eve) pay their compliments while visiting at Cousin Sarah Cray's home in Gary Hundred, a rural South Carolina village in part destroyed during the Civil War. Miss Leontine, who is of a "poetical nature" and "paints sweetly," makes "beautiful afghans"; Miss Polly, who is more "practical" than her sister, has been reduced by the outcome of the war to selling her "elegant" bread and cakes from a "bread-cart." The "timidly virginal" Miss Leontine and the "handsome" Miss Polly take their proper places in an account of Gary Hundred during the Reconstruction that is given in carefully chosen detail, down to the reading tastes of Southern ladies and gentlemen (Miss Leontine likes novels that are "*moral,*" and Judge Abercrombie prefers Montaigne and Lamb to "modern novels"), and to the illiteracy of the local Negro postmaster who begs Eve, since she is "fum de Norf," to read for him the address on a letter mailed from England with its "rudder quare" shape and "diffunt" stamp.

Jupiter Lights abounds in psychological insights of a shrewd nature. Miss Woolson knew her own kind well, as is illustrated on several occasions in the recital of the events in Ferdie Morrison's last days made by Dr. Knox for the benefit of Paul Tennant near the end of the book. In justifying his failure to tell the truth about Morrison to the elderly ladies who admired him, Knox remarks: " 'For good women are awful fools, you know; they are a great deal harder than we are; they think nothing of sending a man to hell; they're awfully intolerant' " (339). A few moments later, Knox concludes his account: " 'Faults and all, he was the biggest kind of a trump, wasn't he? Drunkards are death to the women—to the wives and mothers and sisters; but some of 'em are more lovable than lots of the moral skinflints that go nagging about, saving a penny, and grinding everybody but themselves. The trouble with Ferdie was that he was born without any conscience, just as some people have no ear for music; it was a case of heredity . . .' " (339). In this instance, one cannot help thinking that Miss Woolson was expressing her own views through the medium of the character.

At any rate, her sincere effort to treat dipsomania intelligently in a work of fiction suggests both her interest in certain aspects of modern psychology and her willingness to deal with such material in her art. In this sense at least, *Jupiter Lights* belongs in an American tradition that includes Charles Brockden Brown, Poe, Simms, Hawthorne, and Melville in the ante-bellum period, and Howells and James, among others, in the period after the war. Certainly, one of the best things in the whole novel is the swiftly moving chapter in which Cicely comes to Eve in the dead of night to tell her that Morrison is having one of his spells. The narrative moves swiftly after this. "Ferdie, half dressed and carrying a lighted candle, appeared, his eyes fierce and fixed, his cheeks flushed. At that moment his beauty was terrible; but he saw nothing, heard nothing; he was like a man listening to something afar off" (98). From that moment on, he pursues the two women and the child like a phantom; and though they take every advantage of house and terrain, he appears to materialize near them in their every hiding place and "the yellow gleam of the candle" lights "the beautiful, cruel face" and "the fixed eyes" that do not see them but somehow pursue them. Finally, Eve and the others reach the Sound and the comparative safety of a "row-boat," but Cicely cannot launch it. Thinking to divert Morrison's attention, Eve remains some distance from the shore, but the child's crying and his efforts to disengage himself from his fainting mother attract the dipsomaniac.

> Ferdie saw him; his shoulders made a quick movement; an inarticulate sound came from his flattened, grimacing mouth. Then he began to run towards the boat. At the same moment there was the crack, not loud, of a pistol discharged very near. The running man lunged forward and fell heavily to his knees; then to the sand. His arms made one or two spasmodic movements. Then they were still [102].

The next movement comes from Eve as she races to the shore, gets in the boat, and pushes it with an oar out into the safety of the water.

The contemporary critical reaction to *Jupiter Lights* was not on the whole very favorable, though the book sold well enough at the time. Horace E. Scudder's review in the *Atlantic* in January, 1890, is a case in point. The novel, he remarks, is "somewhat disturbing." "We do not find," he continues, "the best of Miss Woolson in it except in the portraiture of the minor characters and in one strong theme, which is indeed the central theme of the book, but so confused with other issues as to be less effective, we think, than if it had been allowed a simpler expression." As if this were not enough, Scudder was even more concerned that "Miss Woolson's interest in casuistry and her ingenuity of invention are leading her farther and farther away from large pictures of human life into the windings and turnings of fictitious pathology."

This note was also sounded in other places. A writer in the *Critic* for February 1, 1890, agreed in general with the *Atlantic's* reviewer. "The book throughout shows strength," he writes, "but with a tendency to the morbid. One of the characters has homicidal impulses when drunk; another, his wife, is subject to fits of insanity; the heroine is gloomy and incomprehensible, and her successful lover a respectable piece of machinery." This critic, like Scudder, liked the minor characters, "most" of whom, he acknowledged, "are well sketched and amusing."

Miss Woolson was troubled by some of the criticism of *Jupiter Lights*. On April 17, 1890, she remarked on another review of the novel in a letter to Samuel Mather: "Somebody has taken the pains to send me, very carefully directed, a *N. Y. Evening Post*, containing a savage attack upon *Jupiter Lights*; as the *Post* & the *Nation* are the same, the article will go into the *Nation* also, I suppose. . . . But the Post attack touched me a little, because I think it *may* come—in spirit—from Mr. Howells, who, strange to say, has turned from a friend into an enemy. He is powerful; & he is on the spot; & he dislikes with a vengeance! when he does dislike" (Richardson, 19).

More recent critics have, as one may suspect, accepted Miss Woolson's psychological study for what it is and have been more concerned about other aspects of the novel. Kern, for example, points out that the book offers "another excellent picture of the desolation that had overtaken" the South during the period of Reconstruction, but he also comments that the story "becomes less real and more melodramatic as it proceeds" and deplores the "authorial manipulation" that leads to "the conventional happy ending." He concludes that *Jupiter Lights* "is of interest chiefly because it gives a certain unity to Miss Woolson's work by treating, somewhat sketchily and not quite successfully, the three geographical sections with which the author is identified" (92).

Quinn's general view of the work is more favorable than Kern's. The problem of form, one infers from his discussion, is not paramount since "the characters dominate the scene." Some of the action he finds "too melodramatic" ("especially the final scenes in Italy"), but he concludes: "It is, however, a fine study of the havoc made by any woman who tries to manage another's life" (340). Alexander Cowie also remarks on this point: "the chief power of *Jupiter Lights*," he avers, "derives from the concentrated study of troubled personal relations, being in this case a study of a woman who interfered disastrously in the affairs of another." And, he goes on to say, "it is precisely in the mental struggles of persons involved in such cases of casuistry [that is, Eve's ethical problem concerning her part in Morrison's death] that Miss Woolson, like James, succeeds most notably." But, he decides, "the problem is largely lost in the frequently improbable action, and the book remains her least valuable novel" (575).

In the most recent appraisal of the novel, Edward Wagenknecht touches on Miss Woolson's success in dealing with the "mental struggles" of her characters and relates her work of this sort to that of Henry James. James, he says, "would readily have understood the spiritual torture of Eve Bruce . . . when she falls in love" with Paul Tennant. "Here is the 'Should she tell him?' problem of shopgirl fiction on a new level." Wagenknecht notes, however, that Miss Woolson's shifting of the book's center of interest between Eve and Cicely is "even more troublesome" than had been the frequent changes in point of view between Garda and Margaret in *East Angels* (176-77).

With the chief points made against *Jupiter Lights*, one is likely to agree. It is too melodramatic; it does contain some improbable action; the center of interest does shift at times too precariously between Eve and Cicely; and there is some "authorial manipulation," especially in the matter of a contrived ending. And yet one hesitates to characterize the novel as a complete failure. It contains good material, shows some advances in the author's handling of fast-paced narrative, and marks a sincere effort on her part to do something "different." Moreover, as others have stated, the work offers an excellent picture of a part of the South during Reconstruction; some characters of real vitality; and an examination of psychological matters that is still relevant and of interest today.

The book is not entirely a failure, but it is not an unqualified success either. It is indeed, in some ways, the "strongest" thing that Miss Woolson had done in the way of a novel, but she was not primarily gifted as a writer of action and she always had to fight in her long fiction a strong tendency towards the episodic. There is, as a matter of fact, evidence in Miss Woolson's long fiction to indicate her interest in the relationship between it and drama. In *Jupiter Lights,* for example, chapters often begin with a few references to scene: "Fourth of July at Port aux Pins; a brilliant morning with the warm sun tempering the cool air, and shining on the pure cold blue of the lake" (201). Others begin with something similar to a stage description of a change in character: "Eve's cheeks showed a deep rose bloom; she was no longer the snow-white woman whom near-sighted Miss Sabrina had furtively scanned upon her arrival at Romney six months before. She was still markedly erect, but her step had become less confident, her despotic manner had disappeared. Often now she was irresolute, and she had grown awkward—a thing new with her; she did not know how to arrange her smallest action, hampered by this new quality" (159-60). Such devices tend to underscore the episodic nature of part of the novel.[10]

Despite these strictures, *Jupiter Lights* holds its own pretty well in relation to Miss Woolson's other novels. In comparison with *Anne*, for instance, it is less episodic and the action is handled more skillfully, though *Anne* has a freshness and a vitality beyond the limits of the later work. *Horace Chase,* on the other hand, is better constructed and more unified in scope and action than its immediate predecessor among Miss Woolson's works. But one is most of all impressed with the achievement made in *Jupiter Lights* when he reads other American novels published in 1889. Beyond Howells' *Annie Kilburn* and Clemens' *A Connecticut Yankee,* there is little in the way of long fiction in that year that may be compared favorably with *Jupiter Lights.* It is only when one comes to consider the better works of the major writers of this period that Miss Woolson's work begins to take on perspective and to appear as it is—the work of a very talented minor writer of great integrity. It is in this light that *Jupiter Lights* should be read and judged.

V *Horace Chase*

Horace Chase, the last of Miss Woolson's novels, appeared first as a serial in ten issues of *Harper's* beginning in January, 1893, and was brought out as a book by the House of Harper in the early part of 1894. The title of the work suggests that it is centered in the character of Horace Chase, a young self-made millionaire of thirty-eight whose rise from a humble beginning has been based on the American virtues of hard work and a genius for organization.[11] Also taking an important part in the action are the Franklins, a Northern family that had settled at Asheville, North Carolina, a year after the close of the Civil War, and especially Ruth, the youngest daughter, whose guileless and naïve self-centeredness leads her to marry Chase despite the disparity between their ages. The relationship between Ruth and Chase is of central importance to the novel, yet Miss Woolson's approach to it leads to some ambiguity regarding the book's center of interest. Though she stoutly maintained on several occasions that Chase was the "principal personage," the story is told chiefly from the point of view of Ruth Franklin. For this reason (Miss Woolson readily admitted that she was reluctant to describe "the masculine mind"), the reader may easily miss the author's intention and therefore miss some of the things she is trying to say. Thus, as in *East Angels,* there exists the possibility of confusion about the novel's focus, though there is no real difficulty insofar as contrast and situation and character analysis are concerned.

The plot may be readily outlined. The Franklins—a mother and two daughters and an older son—have been left in straitened circumstances by the sudden death of the husband and father, the owner and editor of a newspaper in a town on the Hudson River in New York. Since Mrs. Franklin owned property in Asheville and in St. Augustine, Florida, a bequest from her Huguenot mother's sister, she moved her family to North Carolina in 1866. There, in 1873, the action begins. Horace Chase has come to Asheville to try the "mountain air" and, shrewd businessman that he is, he immediately sees the need for a railroad and the possibilities of the town as a resort. His lack of sophistication and his ample means attract Ruth Franklin, who soon agrees to become his wife. The marriage solves many of the family's financial problems, but Mrs. Franklin, Jared, and Dolly (the invalid elder daughter) cannot help characterizing Chase as *nouveau riche* and as somewhat common. Despite their supercilious attitude toward him, he continues to make money and to care for their financial needs, though Jared declines any direct help from him.

In the course of spending a winter in St. Augustine, Ruth meets and falls desperately in love with Walter Willoughby, an ambitious young New Yorker eager to make his fortune quickly by sharing in Chase's latest enterprise. Unaware of his wife's infatuation, Chase agrees to take on Willoughby as a junior partner and sends him to California to tend the company's interests there. Ruth, never having been denied anything either by her family or by her husband, undergoes a struggle with her love for Willoughby during his absence of two years. Just as she appears to be winning it, he turns up again in St. Augustine. When she discovers that she still loves him, she leaves with Dolly (who is aware of her feelings) for Asheville. Shortly thereafter she sees Willoughby riding into town and decides that she can no longer deny her love for him. Since Chase is in Chicago on business, Ruth leaves home early in the morning while Dolly is still sleeping and seeks out Willoughby in his borrowed lodge in the near-by mountains. Coming to the lodge through the cover of a thicket, she discovers that Walter has guests in the persons of Marion Barclay and her mother and, moreover, that he and Miss Barclay are engaged to be married. Stricken to the heart, she leaves without being seen and is caught in a sudden autumnal storm. Meanwhile Dolly has surmised that Ruth has surreptitiously gone to Willoughby and has followed her. She finds Ruth drenched and dazed and takes her to a mountain home to rest and spend the night.

There they are joined by Chase, who had returned to Asheville to discover that his wife and sister-in-law were not at home. A little deduction leads him to their refuge. He arrives not suspecting that Ruth has had any notion of being unfaithful to him, but she quickly and bluntly tells him all, despite Dolly's objections and rationalizations. Horace is shocked and hurt, but he magnanimously accepts his part of the responsibility for the treatment of Ruth as a child and refuses to judge her. When she realizes that he now accepts her as a woman and wife indeed, she goes to him. The reader is left to conclude that their marriage has at last some foundation upon which to build.

Fortunately for those who wish to study *Horace Chase*, Miss

Woolson has left an account of her plan of the novel in a letter of June 30 [1892?] to Henry Mills Alden. After remarking that "the man is intended to be more important than the woman" and acknowledging the difficulty a woman faces in describing the "masculine mind," Miss Woolson proceeds to outline her plot. When she gets to that point where Chase discovers Ruth and Dolly in a mountain home, she goes into some detail:

> The wife is upstairs, asleep at last—confronted unexpectedly by the husband, the sister, with the inspiration of love, invents upon the spot a perfect explanation of why they are there; i.e., she and her sister. The husband accepts it without hesitation, and sits down to rest by the fire until his wife wakes. The sister meanwhile, starts upstairs, wakens the wife, tells her that her husband is below, and repeats to her what she has told him. Then she urges her not to contradict the story, and her arguments are 1st: that it (the truth) will make him implacably hostile. 2d: that she, the wife has actually done no wrong, since no one on earth knows the motive of her flight, & no one has seen her; and the man whom she intended to join has not the least suspicion of her intention, and will now never know it. 3rd: that she (the wife herself) is now cured of her belief that this second man had ever cared for her, and, in his heartlessness, her own love for him—such as it was—will vanish, has already vanished.
>
> To these arguments the young wife's reply is simply to rise, and go down to her husband—followed by the trembling defeated sister.
>
> The wife then tells the exact truth. Not because she is brave or high-minded. She is neither especially. But because she feels that she must tell it, and therefore the sooner it is over the better.
>
> And when she has got it out (in a few brief phrases), Horace Chase says something like this. 'Go?' (For she has offered to go.) 'Why, where should you go but home? Come back, poor child, and we'll do the best we can. I don't know that I have been so perfect myself, that I have any right to judge you.'
>
> The whole book, as you will see, lies in that last sentence. Do you think it impossible? I do not [Kern, 93-94].

Thus Miss Woolson makes clear her intention, and once again a magnanimous gesture is crucial to the outcome of her story. In this instance the generosity comes from a leading male character, as had been the case much earlier in "Castle Nowhere" and "'Bro'."

That the novel is primarily a study of social relations hinging on Ruth's compulsion to tell the "exact truth" and Horace's generous response is quite evident from Miss Woolson's sketch of the plot. But she also makes some further comments in the same letter to Alden that not only provide some insight into her thinking about other aspects of the work but also suggest some of the restrictions she imposed upon herself:

> I must mention that there are no cave scenes; the infatuation of the young wife with the second man is sketched very lightly, and not dwelt upon. For, in my own mind, Horace Chase is the principal personage. He is a careful study from actual life, although, even in his case, I don't describe so much what he thinks, as what he says, and does. The date is 1873-1876. The two scenes are Asheville, North Carolina (in the mountains), as it was at that time. And St. Augustine, ditto. Both places mentioned by name, and described *realistically*. There are minor characters, and a good deal of fun in the first parts [94].

As the last of her novels, *Horace Chase* clearly reflects Miss Woolson's ever-growing conception of the art of the novel and of her mastery over certain aspects of technique. Indeed, this novel is shorter (419 pages in book form) and more carefully constructed than either *Anne* (540 pages) or *East Angels* (591 pages). The plot and characters are on the whole more fully developed (though the major characters are less fully analyzed) than in *For the Major* (208 pages). The point of view in *Horace Chase,* is still basically omniscient, but there are fewer comments expressed through the narrator and fewer interruptions in the narrative despite the author's propensity towards dialogue and description.

In other words, in her last work the author has detached herself more than ever from the telling of her story without divorcing herself completely from it. As Miss Woolson pointed out with regard to Chase's character in her letter to Alden, there is much less effort to analyze the characters and their motives as fully as in *Anne* or *East Angels*; and thus the narrative moves forward more swiftly, impeded only occasionally by lengthy passages of conversation or description. The ending itself is rather romantically conceived when one considers the author's general views on realism. There is little in Ruth's character to prepare the reader adequately for her sudden response to Chase's magnanimity, but the subtle use of suggestion at this point mitigates to some extent the effect of her apparent change of heart. Finally, there is less attention given to detailed description of locale in *Horace Chase* than in earlier novels. The characters move from the North Carolina mountains to the Florida beaches with less background sketched in by the artist than one finds, say, in *Anne* or *East Angels*. The customs and manners and speech peculiarities of some of the characters are introduced but seldom developed as had been the case in much of Miss Woolson's local-color fiction.

In regard to the characters themselves, they follow the patterns established by the author in her other novels. They are for the most part conceived and developed with an awareness of and concern for proper psychological motivation. The portrait of Ruth Franklin as a young lady whose every emotion motivates her to a naïve concern for her own happiness without regard for the needs of others reminds one of Garda Thorne in *East Angels*; but the picture of Ruth is in some ways more skillfully done. Garda's character is frequently made explicit through detailed descriptions and analyses of her motives and actions. Ruth's is in part suggested and evoked, though the reader is given sufficient information from which to draw conclusions about her qualities as a self-centered young woman.

Many of the other characters are realized with shrewdness, occasional irony, and a keen awareness of human foible and idiosyncrasy. As is usual in Miss Woolson's novels, some of the minor characters are delightfully sketched: Mrs. Franklin, the devoted mother and not-so-devoted mother-in-law; Anthony Etheridge, the land-locked commodore and confirmed old bachelor whose convictions concerning the joys of bachelorhood are sorely tested by the beauties of Mrs. Lilian Kip, a bewitching but slightly bemused widow on the lookout for another husband; Reverend Malachi Hill, an Episcopal missionary whose interest in secular pleasures is illustrated on several occasions; Maud Muriel Mackintosh, a sculptress in the modern manner who likes to make "exact reproductions from life"; and Miss Billy Breeze, a not-so-old maid whose efforts to set her cap for Senator Achilles Larue, a stick-in-the-mud if there ever was one, have always ended in failure.

Among the major characters, Miss Woolson is least successful with Horace Chase himself. His portrait is lacking in something important, and his personality does not emerge with the vitality or naturalness of the author's interpretation of Ruth's character. Since his role, as Miss Woolson has pointed out, is significant in the novel, his characterization becomes a vital matter. The chief difficulty with the character of Chase has to do with his qualities as a businessman. Miss Woolson was well aware of this problem and appealed to her nephew Samuel Mather, a successful businessman in his own right, for advice and suggestions. Mather read portions of the manuscript before it appeared in *Harper's* and made some "corrections" and "improvements," but he could not change the fundamental conception of Chase's character or the method of its development.[12]

The problem is simply this. The reader is told that Chase is a self-made millionaire; but, aside from references to his business trips and enterprises and to his acumen and willingness to work, his qualities as a successful entrepreneur are only vaguely suggested and never really revealed in his character in the novel. One understands Miss Woolson's reasons for handling Chase's character in this way, as one appreciates James's for having done pretty much the same thing with Christopher Newman in *The American*; but the effect on Chase is that of unfulfilled promise. He never is quite what one has a right to expect him to be. Moreover, the action in the novel rarely centers on Horace and his problems except where they concern Ruth and her family. The reader learns almost everything that he knows about Chase from seeing him in some relation or other to the Franklin family. This is not bad in itself, but for a character of Chase's importance this method of characterization is too limited; and, to a novelist of Miss Woolson's standards, the method does less than justice to her usual analytic approach to character study and development.

Thus Chase is neither larger than life nor particularly lifelike in some respects but something less than either. The "fever called living" does not seem to infect him until near the end of the work; and, for one who has had to make his way from a humble beginning and to deal ruthlessly with some of his opponents, this is a telling point. His character is, however, by no means a complete failure. As a man of some commercial vision on the one hand (his view of Asheville and the surrounding country as a resort area anticipates the future, and his plan to endow "scientific research" is farsighted indeed), and as a loving but obtuse and indulgent husband on the other, Chase's character does hit the mark.

In spite of her troubles with her central character, Miss Woolson's sense of humor is as evident as ever. Her lightly ironic treatment of such minor characters as Commodore Etheridge and Mrs. Lilian Kip provides evidence that her vein had not been mined out. One of the most delightful incidents in the novel is Mrs. Kip's party in St. Augustine for the Indians kept imprisoned at Fort San Marco. Hoping to convert the red men to Christianity, Mrs. Kip invites the whole band from the fort to her "afternoon party," although the army officer in charge carefully selects six to represent the others and sends them in company with an interpreter and several "uninvited" soldiers. Mrs. Kip provides dinner for all and then hovers "round her dark-skinned guests":

> When she could not think of anything else to do, she shook hands with them; she had already been through this ceremony eight times. 'If I could only speak to them in their own tongue!' she said, yearningly. And the long sentences, expressive of friendship, which she begged the interpreter to translate to them, would have filled a volume. The interpreter, a very intelligent young man, obeyed all her requests with much politeness. 'Tell them that we *love* them,' said Mrs. Kip. 'Tell them that we think of their *souls*.'
>
> The interpreter bowed; then he translated as follows: 'The white squaw says that you have had enough to eat, and more than enough; and she hopes that you don't make pigs of yourselves if anything else is offered—especially Drowning Raven!' [183-84].

The six Apaches survey the scene impassively even when they are approached by several "serious spinsters" who seek to "have a gentle word with one or two of them, apart" and by Mr. Harrison, a local clergyman, who addresses them with the help of the interpreter whose translation was "a very good speech" itself, though, "perhaps, less spiritual than Mr. Harrison's." The Indians were not edified by any of this "entertainment," but they were impressed with the height of Mrs. Kip's own daughter ("'the young-squaw-with-her-head-in-the-sky'"), who was there to assist her mother in her missionary work.

Miss Woolson worked very hard on *Horace Chase*. In a letter of March 14, 1893, written to Samuel Mather a few weeks before she finished the manuscript of the novel in serial form, she described her plan of work:

> I always write out the whole plot, in every detail, first. Often this takes as much time as to write the book. Then each character is written out, & the amount of paper it covers, for each, is as much nearly as the whole book.—Then come the scenes—at equal length. And finally pages & pages of conversation; incidental only; things that might be said.—All this takes nearly two years! Then comes the terrible putting together; the fitting in the parts. If it were not a serial, it would not be half so much labor. But as I have only a certain fixed amount of space (which I know beforehand), I must first manage to tell my story. And all the rest must be brought in, condensed, to the best advantage. I am aware that I take my work hard. But we must all do as we can, and the only way I can write at all, is to do my very best. Something in me makes me take these enormous pains.

To some extent, this hard work paid off. *Horace Chase* marks an advance in technique and structure over the other novels. But the partial failure in the development of Chase's character mars the "story" and prevents the work from being the satisfying artistic conclusion to Miss Woolson's literary career that it might have been under other circumstances. One can only regret that a book "into which she had put so much of her strength," as Clara Woolson Benedict once remarked, did not more completely fulfill the promise of her earlier novels. The work that might have come after *Horace Chase*—the two or three better novels yet unwritten that she mentioned in one of her last letters and the "substantial contribution" to American fiction that Henry James foresaw in his essay—did not materialize; for Constance Fenimore Woolson died in Italy less than ten days before *Horace Chase* appeared in book form in New York.

CHAPTER 4

The Art of Fiction: Professions of Faith and Practice

THE CHIEF SOURCES for Constance Woolson's ideas on fiction are her essays in the Contributors' Club of the *Atlantic Monthly*; her comments in notebooks and journals, excerpts from which are included in Miss Benedict's *Constance Fenimore Woolson*; and her remarks in letters both published and unpublished. Another presumably important source of her views—her correspondence with Henry James—is apparently not extant (see Chapter I, note 31). Her practice of the art of fiction also provides some insight into her views. In this chapter Miss Woolson's practice is examined mainly to suggest the relationship between it and her theory, and to show some of the literary influences on both these aspects of her fiction.

I *Views of Other Nineteenth-Century Writers of Fiction*

Miss Woolson's thoughts on fiction were based on many years of reading English and French and, later, Italian literature. She read Cooper and Hawthorne and Dickens and Dumas père as she was growing up. *Les Trois Mousquetaires,* she wrote Paul Hamilton Hayne in 1875, was the only book that had ever kept her up "*all* night." She loved Dickens, thought Hawthorne a "god," and admired the romances of her Uncle Fenimore whose work and region she described in an article for *Harper's* in December, 1871. In the same letter to Hayne, she expressed some other opinions: "'Geo. Eliot,' 'Geo. Sand,' and Charles Reade are my favorite living novelists. Of the dead I prefer Charlotte Brontë and Dumas père. . . . Then too there is Victor Hugo. . . . My favorite novel . . . *now* is 'The Mill on the Floss'.

. . . It is the favorite of my mature years." In a letter of September 28, 1874, to E. C. Stedman, she had mentioned some of the same writers: "But Charlotte Brontë, George Eliot, and George Sand are equally powerful with me. Also Dickens." As her tastes developed and matured, she added Turgenev and Henry James to her list, though she maintained her affection for Eliot and Reade throughout her life.[1]

Turgenev she considered the "greatest of modern novelists." She read his work in French and found his technique absorbing. She was particularly impressed by his analysis of character and by his treatment of action in terms of the development of character. The hold his characters had on him (she had heard him described once as "pale, feverish, so changed that he looked like a dying man . . . because the personages of one of his tales had taken such possession of him that he was unable to sleep") brought forth from Constance Woolson a note of understanding and appreciation in a letter to J. L. and J. B. Gilder, the editors of the *Critic* (Benedict, II, 31-32). She read and reread Turgenev's fiction and kept a set of his *Oeuvres* (9 vols., 1880-87) "always in her drawing room." As late as February 24, 1887, she wrote Stedman that she "still" considered Turgenev the "finest by far" of the "great Russians." In her admiration for the Russian artist she belonged to a select contemporary company which included Henry James, Flaubert, and other discriminating practitioners of the art of fiction.

James himself, of course, became her very good friend; but before she went to Europe, she had admired his work and expressed her opinion in anonymous articles printed in the Contributors' Club in the *Atlantic*. Interestingly enough, in July, 1878, she mentioned James and Turgenev together in a discussion of a contemporary novel: "Discussion, even acrid discussion, means strength, I think. The continued arguing of the Contributors' Club over Tourguéneff and Henry James proves that they have strength of some kind, does it not?" Later, in two essays on *The Europeans* (1878) in the January and February issues of 1879, she found much to admire, though she also recognized James's limitations. In the first place, she notes that he "has advanced in his art," for in this work "there is absolutely no action at all. What is there, then?" she asks. "There is contrast of character, and conversation." But there is even more. His "delightful style," she asserts, "is even more delightful than usual in this story" and makes the reader "for a while, impatient with less artistic stories."

On the other hand, she points out the author's shortcomings, especially in regard to certain characters. Felix she characterizes as a "failure," or rather a "shadow," since he makes "no definite impression of any kind"; she also chastises James for his "unregenerate" attitude toward Mr. Brand: and, finally, she opines that James is not "quite fair" in his first description of the Baroness' "personal appearance" because he follows Turgenev and pictures "the irregularities of her features and personal deficiencies so minutely" that one can never "forget" and "think of her as in the least handsome." This is wrong, Miss Woolson believes, because the Baroness is indeed "handsome"—an "extremely charming woman" of a sort one is likely to meet in "real life"; that is, she is a woman of "irregular features" who nevertheless wins attention because of "some one single and wonderfully great beauty."

Despite these strictures, Miss Woolson in her second essay on James, characterizes *The Europeans* as a "perfect work of its kind, and delightful reading to those whom such study interests." Then she takes up a point made against James in his own day and later as well, and shrewdly answers it in a way calculated not only to defend James but any author (including herself) vitally interested in character analysis. Her remarks on this matter bear quoting in full:

> But among his admirers are many who complain of him as a disappointing author—one who charms their interest from the first, and keeps it alive to the end, but who, at the end, is apt to leave them somewhat dissatisfied. The conclusions of his novels and tales, they say, seem to them a breaking off rather than a true finishing of the lives and fortunes of the personages he has made them acquainted with. He gives reality and vitality to his characters only to make the reader close the book, asking, Is that all about them? It is not enough, or not the end they should come to. This is a reproach, it seems to me, applicable to many weaker authors, less skilled in their art, but not to Mr. James. In his case the apparent failure to come to anything particular is foreseen by the author himself, because it is inherent in the nature of the theme chosen. It is certainly evident that the author of *Roderick Hudson* and *The American* has not the genuine story-telling gift, the power of inventing a story interesting for its own sake. His talent lies in another field, that of keen observa-

> tion and fine discrimination of character, which he portrays with a subtle and delicate touch. It is unreasonable, I think, to complain of a writer for not being something else than he is, as it would be to find fault with a figure painter that he was not a landscape artist. When we have once recognized the quality of a man's talent, why not take what he can give, and not ask for something different? Let us do without a story in Mr. James's novels, and enjoy instead something certainly as admirable in its way. Observing the refined skill with which the contrast of typical characters is presented in *The Europeans,* I, for one, was not disposed to demand a more exciting dénoument, the interest of each page as I read it being pleasure sufficient.

This passage suggests the quality of Miss Woolson's insight into and appreciation of James's early work; aside from Howells, few critics in the 1870's gave James such a discriminating reading. It is all the more remarkable when one considers that she had been "very much disappointed" in *Roderick Hudson* and that she was not one to scorn the value of plot.

Miss Woolson also liked James's short stories; "two or three" of them she thought better than anything else he had done with the exception of *The Europeans,* but Bret Harte's work in the genre was more meaningful to her in the 1870's. As Pattee has remarked in the *Development of the American Short Story* (1923), "the influence of Harte upon her work was at first considerable" (252). Her first sketches reveal her interest in locality—the lake country and Ohio—and some of her better early stories take up several themes Harte had recently advanced in his fiction. In both "The Lady of Little Fishing" (1874) and "Castle Nowhere" (1875), there is the motif of "The Luck of Roaring Camp"; in "Castle Nowhere" there is also the theme of self-sacrifice developed in a way not unlike that in "The Outcasts of Poker Flat." Furthermore, in "Misery Landing" (1874) the central character, a man of culture, tries to educate an ignorant boy by reading Harte (and other authors) aloud to him; later the cultured man writes in his journal that "there is more of goodness and generosity and courage" in Harte's words "than in many a sermon."

Harte's name also occurs frequently in Miss Woolson's letters, but she is chary of acknowledging the dimensions of his influence. In a letter of September 28, 1874, to Stedman, for instance, she touched on this matter: "In spite of all I said to you, I do *not* plead guilty to imitating Harte. I only meant that his style had impressed me so deeply that it would be a wonder if something did not show to others how much he was to me. But Charlotte Brontë, George Eliot, and George Sand are equally powerful with me. Also Dickens. Harte coming last was the sensation of the hour, that was all." Two years later she mentioned Harte again in another letter to Stedman: "I am sorry about Bret Harte's play. And I am afraid to read 'Gabriel Conroy'; I skimmed a little of it, and it seemed so disappointing. I cannot desert my old favorite; but I think I shall read no more of his later work, but confine myself to the sketches which first won my admiration."

At the same time she wrote Hayne: "I have an inner fondness, I think, for the 'striking.' I am obliged to keep the balance straight by reading quantities of such writings as Lamb's, etc." "How savage are the critics over Bret Harte's play!" she observed later in the same letter. "But they all hate him," and she added: "He is *not* a nice person, I am told." Years later, however, in the early 1890's, Harte's early short stories were still a standard for her, and when she measured the tales of a "young fellow" named Kipling against them, she found "Ruddy's" pieces wanting and commented in a letter to Miss Guilford: "They are original, and strong after a fashion. Still I am disappointed. They do not, in my opinion, equal Bret Harte's early tales. But of course the English are much struck with them as they have not many Bret Hartes."

One may question whether Harte was in any way instrumental in stimulating Miss Woolson to write in the first place or in turning her interest to locality. She wrote obviously and naturally about what she knew and had observed. But there is little doubt that her reading of Harte and her reaction to his "deep-hearted prose" stimulated her work after its beginnings and gave it direction until she departed for Europe in 1879.

II *Realism*

Harte was certainly among those older writers whose work led Miss Woolson towards realism, though, at the same time, his particular brand of romanticism also made its mark on her fiction. Her interest in the history and natural scenery of Mackinac, the Great Lakes region, and the South led her to read much and to observe carefully. The results of her study and examination she recorded in fiction that faithfully evoked a sense of time and place, but she was too much a creature of her day not to treat her materials within the limits prescribed by a view of life she held in common with many of similar backgrounds and traditions. She had a penchant for the "striking" she once wrote Hayne; she also admired the soul capable of self-sacrifice and the themes of magnanimity and renunciation. These views manifested themselves in various ways in her fiction, and they on occasion led her to mix large elements of romanticism with her realism, though she considered herself a realist. "I am very fond of 'the real'," she informed Hayne once, "almost too much so, I fear." She had certain reservations about an extreme realism, however, which she described in her notebooks:

> Story writers who have eyes and ears (occasionally noses—for scents); but no imagination, or soul; or else, while possessing these last, they rigidly keep them down, not allowing them to enter at all into their literary work. Such writers produce a photographic and phonographic copy of real life as it is on the surface. But is this correct? Is such a copy accurate? Do we interpret our mother, our child, our husband, our wife, by simply what each actually does or says? Have we not, under each act, a thousand intuitions that modify it, or even falsify it? Don't we know that they do not mean this or that because of our under-knowledge of their character? [Benedict, II, 97].

In one of her last letters to Stedman, written on August 10, 1889, she took up the problem again: "In your letter, you touch upon the vexed questions of realism and idealism. . . . Over here, one reads so constantly French, Russian, Spanish, & Italian novels . . . that one can't be much of a partisan about anything; the field seems so wide, & there's something good in all. I am a realist. But that does not make me believe that only bad, or commonplace, characters exist. I *know* to the contrary."[2]

Coming from Miss Woolson, such an assertion does not seem unreasonable when one considers the scope of her fiction, though a reader of the mid-twentieth century may be excused for thinking that she frequently concentrated her attention on "good" or "uncommonplace" characters. She justified this attention in the same letter to Stedman: "As to my Margaret in 'East Angels' (to which you allude), I have known just such a woman; & more than one."[3] Thus she marks the relationship between personal experience and reality, and one should remember that her view of realism—"All I write is founded, and intended to be founded, upon actual realities. I have no interest in anything else"—was based on her limited experience, which was as circumscribed in its way as was James's.

Not without merit is Pattee's view that "she posed as a realist" but was actually a "poet" who "worked always with selected materials" which "demanded heavy lights and shadows" and that her "Cooper-like imagination" led her to idealize her materials. But this is not the whole story. She does, as James points out, "like a glamour," but, he continues, "she usually succeeds in producing a valid one." She does often "purge" her materials of grossness or treat circumspectly matters that later writers deal with forthrightly, but this does not mean that she has thereby produced something unreal. She has simply chosen to concentrate on certain virtues rather than on certain vices—as some realists have done. Though this emphasis may lead modern readers to think that her work is not in proper balance, it does not lessen its validity as a restricted view of life within the context of her own time.[4] At the same time, this restricted view does "date" her work and limit the universality of its appeal. Still, her examination of character on the basis of psychological analysis and a study of motives ("I care only for motives," she observed in a notebook once; "why a man or woman does or has done so and so") gives her fiction a realistic aspect that should for readers of the twentieth century mitigate some of its dated qualities.

III *The Influence of James and Howells*

Her efforts to examine the "mental states" of her characters and her interest in the international theme led many of Miss Woolson's contemporaries—and later critics as well—to associate her work with that of James and Howells. E. C. Stedman, for example, pointed out the relationship in a letter of November 12, 1882: "Your imagination is more *creative* than Howells's or James's—follow your own bent, give us life and passion and color, and do not, like them, overdo your 'analysis' and 'subtilties'." Twenty-five years later he still thought of her accomplishment in terms of the achievement of Howells and James. Contemporary critics have related her work especially to that of James. Many see her as a "follower" of the master, a view that Kern has shared, though he has admitted that he could find "no direct evidence of indebtedness on either side" (178). Lyon N. Richardson asserts that she is clearly in James's debt: "As her portrayal of purely sectional characteristics grew less pronounced in her novels and later short stories, she took increased interest in contrast of character, in situation, and in analysis of qualities. In all these things she followed James" (19). Van Wyck Brooks in *The Times of Melville and Whitman* (1947) also characterizes Miss Woolson, among other things, as a "reader and follower of James . . . and Turgenev. . ." (349).

Other critics have not been so sure of James's influence. Pattee in his "Constance Fenimore Woolson and the South" points out that, though Miss Woolson and James appear to be "in accord in their art ideals," her fiction is "not greatly . . . influenced" by his. "Her art methods," he explains, were already "hardened into habit" when "she first encountered him." "Yet," he admits, "much in her fiction reminds us of James's manner" (140). Cowie, though aware of the similarity in the views regarding fiction held by these two, nevertheless concludes that Miss Woolson made her own contribution in the heroines she created. "It was finally these heroines who inspired most of what was distinguished in the work of Constance Fenimore Woolson. She described their persons with a critical eye, understood the crises of their 'private relations' with fine intuition, recorded their self-immolations with a quiet intensity that often lends exaltation to her page" (578).

A more recent commentator, Edward Wagenknecht, describes in his *Cavalcade of the American Novel* (1952) some of the literary ways in which James and Miss Woolson resemble each other: "It was natural that James should admire Miss Woolson. Both were devoted to Turgenev; both favored impressionism and the dramatic method; both cultivated the virtues of detachment. Her notebooks are not altogether unlike his. They were alike too in their preoccupation with the nuances of human character and with nice problems of conscience" (176). But Wagenknecht does not suggest that any master-disciple relationship existed between the two writers.

Though the critics do not agree on the extent of the influence of Howells and James on Constance Woolson, it is clear that their work influenced hers to a degree. She once wrote Howells, for example, that he was one of her three "classics" in regard to "style,"[5] and her interest in James's work in the 1870's has already been discussed. Two or three points, however, should be suggested about the nature and extent of this influence. In the first place, in the matter of analysis and treatment of character, Miss Woolson had read George Eliot before she came to admire the work of James or Howells, and she had read Turgenev with care before either American writer had much influence on her own fiction. Both Eliot and Turgenev exerted important influences on Miss Woolson's work, as she herself said on a number of occasions. They also greatly influenced the early work of Henry James, and Turgenev was one of Howells' "literary passions." It seems reasonable to assume, then, that some of the resemblances between the fiction of James and Miss Woolson (especially those concerning treatment of character and technique) occur not as a result of the direct influence of the one writer on the other but stem from the common nourishment each had received from George Eliot and Turgenev.

In the second place, in regard to her interest in the international theme, Miss Woolson from the very beginning of her career was fascinated by the impingement of the culture of the Old World on the New. Her stories and sketches dealing with the Great Lakes country and her pieces with Florida backgrounds frequently reveal this interest, as Brooks has pointed out. It is not strange, then, that she became interested after her arrival in Europe in a theme that had appealed to her from another point of view in America—the contrast of the New World with the Old and the treatment of American characters in an Old World setting. That James and Howells had already done this successfully does not mean that she took up the theme in order to emulate them, although their success may have encouraged her to follow her own natural inclination.

At any rate, she addressed herself to this theme in the 1880's, but never in quite the same way as her contemporaries; for she did not treat it in the novel (though she frequently placed Northerners in a Southern context in her long fiction of this period), and her point of view in her stories is limited in scope and so thoroughly American that her work in this vein seems less cosmopolitan than that of either James or Howells. When, for instance, Hamilton W. Mabie proposed in 1883 that she write a novel with a European background, she candidly replied:

> I am afraid I shall hardly be able to write upon a European background—as you suggest. The moment I take up my pen, the old home-scenes are all I ever see; I see them so vividly that I can see nothing else. I have a theory, too, that those of us who remember the war—who were old enough to be stirred by it, yet, at the same time, young enough to have it the first great event of our lives—we, of that generation, are the most deeply-dyed 'Americans' that exist. . . . And so though I should stay years over here, I remain as I was when I first landed; and American scenes—at least in serious work—are all, I fear, that you will ever have from me.[6]

In April of the same year she had written Stedman on the same subject:

> . . . I am so American! I didn't know it until I came over here. I see, now, that, though I should stay in Italy ten years longer, I should never be anything but American; should never write any but the most 'American' prose. The reason is—not that I do not appreciate all the beauty here; I do; I adore it. But because I have lived my life there before I came over. All the deep feelings of my existence are inseparably associated with home-scenes—'scenes,' too having always been in themselves a great deal to me—I don't know why. The Lake-Country & Mackinac, the beautiful South, the farming-country of Ohio—these are the scenes that I belong to, that I can never separate myself from—though I should live years in Venice and Rome.

And yet, despite these sentiments in behalf of home, Miss Woolson had begun writing stories with European backgrounds in 1880, and all of her subsequent short fiction deals with American characters in a European scene.

On the whole, in regard to the relationship between her work and that of James and Howells, one might do well to consider carefully James's *Partial Portraits* (1888). He chose, surely with good reason, to include his essay on Constance Fenimore Woolson with ones discussing George Eliot, Ivan Turgenev, and "The Art of Fiction." That he also included essays on Emerson, Stevenson, and Maupassant, among others, should not deter one from noting the relationship thus suggestively established between Miss Woolson's work and that of George Eliot and Turgenev.

IV *Matters of Technique: Themes*

In matters of technique Miss Woolson is not always quite so successful as her great contemporaries. The themes running through her novels and sketches often stress various aspects of a nobility of character achieved through self-denial, renunciation, magnanimity, or "heroic sacrifice," to use James's term. Such expressions of strength of character appealed to her in a vital way, for they reflect to an important extent the high ideals by which she tried to live her own life. She was, however, also well aware of the relationship that obtains between pride, self-satisfaction, and obtuseness on the one hand and magnanimity on the other, as any reader who has followed the adventures of Eve Bruce in *Jupiter Lights* can readily attest. "Self-denial," she says in her notebooks, "is giving up what one really likes. Search for the secret taste of each person, and see if *that* is indulged! If it is, there is no self-denial, no matter how ascetic the man (or woman) may appear to be." After pointing out that there is a "difference between the evil to others which certain sins and indulgences cause," she continues:

> But leaving the danger to *others* aside, why should an inveterate smoker consider himself so superior to the drunkard? Why should a gormandizer and an epicure, ditto? Each is indulging what happens to be his strongest taste. It is no self-denial to one man to go without meat; but to give up buying rare books would kill him—nearly. One man must have a good horse. Another must have a good dinner. When self-denial is the question, let each look within [Benedict, II, 110].

Of course, Miss Woolson did not hesitate to vary this theme. In her early work, she developed it from a somewhat Harte-like point of view: that there is good—nay, perhaps nobility—even in the so-called "outcasts" of society. This is certainly true in "Castle Nowhere" and in "The Lady of Little Fishing," but the reverse—there may be no good in some outcasts—is also true in "Peter the Parson," a tale written at about the same time.

There were other themes too that attracted her attention. Her interest in the international theme has already been discussed from two points of view. One of her most interesting themes involves the aftermath of the Civil War in the South, and some of her best stories—"Rodman the Keeper," "Old Gardiston," "In the Cotton Country," and "King David"—deal effectively with Reconstruction in the defeated Confederacy. Both Pattee and Brooks have maintained that her best work was done in her Southern sketches, and surely there is much to support this view. She wrote Hayne in 1876 that she had tried to put herself in the Southern position and "at least be fair" in her point of view. James remarked on this empathic stance in his essay on her work: "She loves the whole region, and no daughter of the land could have handled its peculiarities more indulgently, or communicated to us more of the sense of close observation and intimate knowledge" (180).

Another point should be made in regard to Miss Woolson's interest in the postwar South. The aftermath of the great event in her life would doubtless have appealed to her imagination under other circumstances, but in this instance she was moved by the spirit of the Southern people in the midst of adversity and by the dramatic contrast between the remains of a destroyed way of life and the beginnings of another way struggling to be born. This contrast (and contrast in its various manifestations is always a theme with Constance Woolson) stirred her to take pen in hand, and her sympathy for the defeated land and people led her to seek to understand their plight and to try to be fair in handling her materials. That she was able to treat the fallen enemy compassionately in her stories of the 1870's is all the more remarkable when one considers, as she observed to Hayne in 1876, "that the beaten track was all the other way." One has only to contrast her work with that of her fellow New Englander John W. De Forest, for example, to appreciate the justice of her remark. She was indeed, as Hubbell has pointed out in *The South in American Literature*, "the earliest Northern writer of fiction who after the war treated Southern life with sympathy and knowledge" (735).

The life of the artist and artistic integrity also appealed to Miss Woolson as thematic material. In several stories she dealt with one aspect or another of artistic integrity, as James was doing in his tales and nouvelles on a larger scale and in a much more definitive way. Variations of this idea appear in three of her better short stories—"Miss Grief" (1880); "The Street of the Hyacinth" (1882); and "In Sloane Street" (1892).[7] In the first of these, the central character is an American woman who has come to Rome to seek advice regarding her unproduced drama from a financially successful American expatriate writer, who is in some respects not unlike Henry James. She refuses to accept her counselor's proffered advice which would, in effect, destroy the integrity of her crude but powerful work; finally, she dies of privation. "The Street of the Hyacinth" varies the theme, for artistic integrity is only indirectly involved, but integrity of character is a matter of concern; and, once again, the leading male character, in his knowledge of art and literature, resembles James.

" 'In Sloane Street'," as Kern has said, "is even more similar than 'Miss Grief' to James's 'Lesson of the Master' " (149). The only one of Miss Woolson's stories to have a London setting, the situation revolves around a writer whose wife is interested in her husband's career for purely financial reasons and whose friend (in this instance a female, in contrast to the admiring young male of James's tale) wishes him to fulfill his promise as an author. Complications involving a child are introduced (and again one is reminded of the Jamesian work), but Miss Woolson's writer appears less serious about his work than James's author and the ensuing development ends in a denouement quite different from that in "The Lesson of the Master" (1888).

To appreciate Miss Woolson's choice of themes, one might do well to consider briefly those she did *not* write about. As Richardson has pointed out, "she was restricted in her use of four themes which her feminine contemporaries employed so easily to win popular favor." Her limited "life-experiences" prevented her from writing very much about domestic matters, nor could she "write of life in the factories or of evangelism along the waterfronts." She was not concerned in her fiction with "revaluations of the social and religious concepts fermenting in the minds of the middle class of the latter nineteenth century," and the glorification of "the sex-emancipated woman" was a theme that "violently displeased her."[8] But that she did not treat these themes in her fiction is the result of something more than lack of experience. In the first place, she had little sympathy for them; and a "grain of sympathy," she once remarked in her notebooks, in relation to another matter, is necessary for discovering "the best" there is in something. Moreover, to one of her temperament and taste who believed with Turgenev "in the intrinsic value of 'subject' in art," these themes must have seemed unworthy of the attention of the serious literary artist.

In the final analysis, Miss Woolson did not write except incidentally to promote specific views—social, economic, or otherwise. Nor did she write merely to entertain or edify the reader. She wrote "for the public," as she informed Samuel Mather in 1891, and to make a living. Though she had other means, she wished to live as much as possible on what she made from her work. But she did not view herself as catering to the public taste. When readers chastised her for killing off Peter the Parson in the tale of the same name and for making the reprobate Fog the central character in "Castle Nowhere," she maintained in her letters that from "an artistic and truthful-to-life point of view" her work was sound and that she was not to be "held personally responsible for the theology and morality" of her characters.[9]

She was aware of the problem concerning public taste when she first considered writing a novel, and in several letters written to Hayne in 1875 she wondered how a "barbarian" such as herself ("I have such strong likes and dislikes. And for what I care, nobody else seems to care") could possibly appeal to the public. "But there is one fact that appals me," she observed to Hayne in 1876. "I generally throw half across the room all the new novels of the day. Now these novels the *Public* like! Moral: will they not be likely to throw mine *entirely* across the room? I fear so." Of course, she wrote her novel anyway and it became popular, but she never prostituted her art simply to appeal to the public or to make money. One might point out in this regard, for example, that the novels published after *Anne* did not sell so well as *Anne* and that Miss Woolson declined in 1891 the attractive financial offers of four "syndicates" in order to remain with Harper & Brothers, her old publisher. She had artistic reasons for writing as well as pecuniary ones, and therefore she did not let these latter interfere with her efforts to explore the complications of the situations she invented or to examine the motives of the characters who give life to these situations.

V *Characters and Characterization*

In regard to matters of technique other than theme, Miss Woolson concerned herself chiefly with character and characterization, and her practice often clearly reflects the views she expressed in one place or another. "Character," she writes in her notebooks, "should (to be interesting), grow and develop on the scene; in the book." It is not, she concludes, "to be introduced completely formed in the beginning" (Benedict, II, 99). This dictum is particularly true of the principal characters in her best fiction. One thinks immediately of Madam Carroll in *For the Major* and of Margaret Harold in *East Angels,* though occasionally in these works and more frequently in *Anne* and *Jupiter Lights* the growth of character is sometimes equated with the revelation of character by an omniscient author. Thus in the case of Anne Douglas' reaction to the beginnings of the Civil War, the reader is informed before Anne can react as a character in the story that she is "in a measure ignorant of the causes and questions of the great struggle" because she has been brought up "in a remote little community" and that she has neither "the prayerful ardor of the New England girl" nor the "proud loyalty of the Southern girl to her blood and to her State."

Nevertheless, the omniscient point of view seeks in *Anne* and in other fiction as well to examine the minds of the characters and to analyze them for the reader's enlightenment. In *For the Major,* for instance, Sara Carroll's gradual realization that all is not well with her father and that her stepmother is not being candid with her is skillfully handled. The reader looks into Sara's mind with the help of the narrator and learns that it is filled with "trouble composed in equal parts of perplexity, disappointment, and grief" because her father has "turned from her" for reasons she cannot understand.

On the other hand, an important character may analyze himself (though the point of view may be in the third person) and therefore reveal certain aspects of his character by his reaction to other characters. Such is the case with Evert Winthrop in *East Angels* when he misjudges Margaret Harold's motives for surreptitiously visiting Lucian Spenser. "He had always disapproved of Margaret in one way; but at least—so he kept telling himself—at least he had thought her entirely without traits of this kind [that is, a married woman who would keep a clandestine meeting with a man not her husband]. He had thought her cold; but he had thought, too, that she had principles, and strong ones" (386).

Occasionally one character describes or analyzes another, as in the case of Miss Sabrina Abercrombie's first view of Eve Bruce in *Jupiter Lights*. "She saw before her a woman of thirty (as she judged her to be; in reality Eve was twenty-eight), tall, broad-shouldered, slender, with golden hair and a very white face. The eyes were long and rather narrow; they were dark blue in color, and they were not pleasant eyes—so Miss Sabrina thought; their expression was both angry and cold. The cheeks were thin, the outline of the features bold. The mouth was distinctly ugly, the full lips prominent, the expression sullen" (10). There is an even better example of "indirect characterization," as Cowie has pointed out, in the beginning of *Anne*. In the opening dialogue between father and daughter, the reader not only learns something about William Douglas and Anne but through them he is introduced to a third character (Miss Lois Hinsdale) who has not yet made her appearance. "It would be hard," Cowie concludes, "to find in fiction of the time an example of more skilful indirect characterization than is here presented" (571).

Concerning dialogue itself, Miss Woolson not only belongs to her time but is ahead of it. Like James, she became increasingly fond of the dramatic method. She frequently places her characters in a setting, and the ensuing action is based on dialogue between them interspersed with bits of exposition and directions from a point of view devised to give the reader a picture or "scene." Thus, in *East Angels* when Evert Winthrop finally declares his love to Margaret Harold, he comes upon her in a "glade . . . leaning against . . . an old nondescript pillar." She wears "no gloves" and he notices "her pretty hand with its single ring, the band of plain gold." Margaret's response to his declaration is therefore prepared for in this simple way. The scene is then completed: "In front of her there was the low curb of an old well, overgrown with jessamine; she appeared to be looking at it" (538).

As the two talk, bits of stage movement are described: "She had taken her hand from the old pillar, she stood erect now, with the white shawl she was wearing folded closely round her" (539). All is explicit. "She had turned away with bent head." She "sank down" upon "an old stone seat." "She did not look up." "Still she did not move." "She stirred at last, she looked up at him." "She sat there, her eyes on his hard, insistent face." "She got up." "She walked about for a moment or two, and finally stopped, facing him, behind the old stone seat." Thus Margaret's response to Evert's passionate pleas underscores the poignancy of her plight at the same time that the drama of the situation is revealed in her movements. The dialogue itself is likely to sound a bit dated to modern ears. Certainly the diction and rhythm are quite different from anything in Hemingway and Faulkner. Still, Miss Woolson's control over and management of dialogue improved with the passage of time, and the conversation in *Horace Chase* seldom sounds as "stiltedly bookish" (to borrow Pattee's phrase) as some that appears in her early stories.[10]

It is not strange that Miss Woolson should seek to incorporate in her fiction certain aspects of dramatic technique, for she had from an early age enjoyed the drama. As a child she had participated in plays made up by the children in the family; as a young lady she had attended the theater in Cleveland and New York and enjoyed the performances of Joseph Jefferson and Edwin Booth. Later, in England and Europe, she saw Duse and Salvini and Henry Irving and attended a first-night performance of James's *The American* in 1891. She was even tempted to write a play, as she admitted to Stedman in a letter in 1876: "Do not tempt me about writing 'a play.' I have such a strong taste that way already! And I suppose that, knowing nothing practically of the requisites, I should make a complete failure. Very likely I shall write one some day; and then—not print it." Alive to the possibilities of the dramatic method, she commented in January, 1879, in the Contributors' Club on James's habit of using " 'stage directions' " in *The Europeans*. "Thus," she observes, "fourteen times in three consecutive pages, taken at random from those containing conversation, it is particularly noted down that they 'looked at' each other. . . . Generally, in print, *cela va sans dire*. I don't mean that this is a fault at all," she hastens to add, "but certainly it is a characteristic peculiarity" (108). Many years later, in the early 1890's, she and James planned to write a play together. One can only regret that this project never came to fruition.

In respect to the use of point of view, Miss Woolson was not nearly so much concerned with all the niceties and ramifications as was James. She was generally content to deal with her characters and situations from an omniscient point of view. As her career as a novelist developed, she intruded in the action less and less, until in *Horace Chase*, her last novel, one finds little evidence of intrusion. She seldom pauses in her fiction to lecture the reader, though her views on a given topic may be expressed by one of her characters, but these views are expressed in character. Her philosophy of life, as a matter of fact, is expressed in her work, but it is always relevant to the story and characters. In her best stories and novels one is reminded only occasionally of authorial omniscience, and then in a way that is in keeping with the fictional situation. The illusion of reality is seldom destroyed by long asides that break the narrative or by confidential addresses to the reader that interfere with the suspension of his belief in what is going on. The "narrative situation is the thing," as Cowie has pointed out, and Miss Woolson as a careful artist used point of view in ways calculated to facilitate the development of the narrative and the probing of the minds of her characters.

VI *Plot*

As many critics have noted, it is in plot, among the factors of technique, that Miss Woolson is weakest. She was aware of the value of plot, as a passage in one of her later notebooks reveals: "The plot must be a riddle, so as to excite curiosity. My idea is that there should be a riddle and exciting adventures. And *growth* of at least several of the characters, so that one will not be sure beforehand what they will do. An intense realism of description and dramatic action. *And there shall be nobility*" (Benedict, II, 108).

Despite these principles, her novels appear episodic because she often includes extraneous and sometimes melodramatic materials, alternates her focus from one character to another, or moves rapidly from one locale to another. Cowie asserts, for example, that Miss Woolson "never mastered" the structure of a "long narrative." There is some justice in this view, though it might be suggested that *For the Major*, her only novelette, is a carefully constructed "long narrative." Moreover, *Horace Chase*, despite a change of scene, also shows a concern for structure that Cowie himself recognizes when he notes that the novel "marks a return to the narrower scope of action in which Miss Woolson moved with greatest freedom and sureness" (575). As a matter of fact, Cowie readily admits that "at her best" Miss Woolson "concretely illustrates" James's point in "The Art of Fiction" that "a novel is a living thing, all one and continuous, like any other organism, and . . . that in each of the parts there is something of each of the other parts."

It ought also to be said in this regard that Constance Woolson's fiction was prepared first for serial publication in magazines (as indeed was much American fiction of this period) and that her treatment of plot and her use of incident were therefore likely to create, especially in her novels, an episodic effect. She was not unaware of this; in the revisions she always made before a serial was published in book form, she tried to remedy this defect as well as she could. She took revision seriously, as many of her letters indicate, but she was never able to revise drastically enough to eliminate the episodic qualities of *Anne* and *Jupiter Lights*. For the most part, to do so would have been impossible without a complete recasting, particularly of *Anne*. One may suggest that this is a quality peculiar to much serial fiction and not merely to Miss Woolson's novels, but this hardly justifies flaws in structure. For this reason, among others, had Miss Woolson relegated plot to a subordinate position in her work (or dispensed with it altogether), concentrated her attention more completely on her characters, and broadened the field a bit in regard to her choice of themes, she might have anticipated the future more precisely. And her best novels and stories might be read more widely and more often today—at least by the discriminating audience that has taken the work of Henry James to heart.

That she thought she was on the right track, however, is clear from the tenor of the references in her letters to the way she worked. In 1893, for example, she wrote Katharine Livingston Mather: "I was particularly pleased with what you wrote of 'Horace Chase.' I don't suppose any of you realize the amount of time and thought I give to each page of my novels; every character, every word of speech and of description is thought of, literally, for years before it is written out for the final time. It takes such entire possession of me that when, at last, a book is done, I am pretty nearly done myself" (Benedict, II, 52). Such wholehearted dedication aptly describes both the woman and the artist. If Miss Woolson did not live to fulfill the promise James had anticipated, the critic may regret the loss to American fiction, but he must not therefore neglect to acknowledge and evaluate the very real contribution Constance Woolson did make.

CHAPTER 5

The Loss of the Laurel: Literary Reputation

IN HER OWN DAY, Miss Woolson's work was well received by the public, though she was not a "popular" writer in the accepted sense of the term. The critics for the most part respected her standards of artistry and her fiction. Constance Woolson herself had been skeptical in the beginning about whether someone of her "barbarian" views could write a novel acceptable to the public, but *Anne* sold well; and Harper and Brothers responded accordingly by paying her an additional thousand dollars and by offering to pay royalty on the work in book form.[1] Some of the critics were also warm in their praise. A reviewer in *Harper's* (August, 1882), for instance, was impressed by the illusion of reality created by the author and by the humanity of her characters: "In her hands," he asserted, "character is a growth, which . . . reveals itself by admitting us to a sight of the processes of evolution. . . ." *Anne,* he concluded, was superior to Howells' *A Modern Instance* (1881) as "a work of art." Other critics found fault with the plot and the use of "accident" in *Anne,* but even these praised the first part of it, and one concluded that it was an "unusual book."

Her later books, with the exception of *East Angels,* did not sell so well as *Anne,* but her critical reputation grew; and in 1887 Henry James contributed an essay on her work to *Harper's Weekly* that did much to describe and characterize for posterity her contribution to fiction. Twenty years later, in a speech made in New York City for a "Keats-Shelley Entertainment," E. C. Stedman characterized Miss Woolson as "that gifted and noble American woman . . . whose writings with those of James, Howells, and a few others of her generation . . . lifted our imaginative literature throughout a most adverse environment to a proud station of its own" (Stedman and Gould, II, 424).

Since 1907, however, her reputation, like that of Howells after his death, has declined; but, though Howells has enjoyed a recent critical revival, Miss Woolson's work is still for the most part neglected. It has been discussed intermittently, as Kern has pointed out, and there are occasionally "sensitive critics" or "zealous historians" who, according to Cowie, continue to "rediscover" her as a "superior minor writer." She is known, then, chiefly by an academic audience limited in reality to close students of nineteenth-century American literature.[2] To the American reading public of the mid-twentieth century, her work is unknown and her name means nothing.[3]

I *Writer Without Readers*

That this situation is unfortunate goes without saying, but why is Miss Woolson's work not read in her own country, where literary taste is so diverse that hundreds of thousands of readers buy almost indiscriminately everything from Homer to comic books? The most obvious reason, of course, is that her books are out of print. In itself this is not unusual. According to Malcolm Cowley, all of William Faulkner's books were out of print in 1945, and from 1954 until 1961 not one of William Gilmore Simms's more than thirty volumes of fiction was in print. The strange thing is that, in a day given to the publication of paper-bound books in the millions of copies, any American writer of merit should be allowed to go completely out of print.[4]

There are, to be sure, other reasons. Reading tastes have changed considerably and the technique of fiction has improved in such important ways that Miss Woolson's work often appears dated in treatment of themes, characters, and in technical matters; she did have trouble solving the problem of form in her long fiction. Some of her views, for example, sound decidedly Victorian; for the modern reader, her greatest limitation doubtless is her inability to deal frankly and forthrightly with love and sex. This despite the fact that she does not hesitate to treat in a general way in her novels such matters as marital infidelity, as readers of *East Angels* and *Horace Chase* will readily remember. She was aware of this limitation, which becomes all the more important when one considers that romantic love is an ingredient in much of her fiction. In a letter of July 23, 1876, she described her situation to Stedman: "I always steer clear of it ["love-making"] if possible; I am afraid of betraying my ignorance; fancy-sketches, you know, are usually unreal! My idea of love is, unfortunately, so high, that, like my idea of the office of minister, nothing or nobody ever comes up to it." One could hardly find a more candid confession of ignorance and idealism than this!

Yet, considered by itself, this failure to deal adequately with "love-making" in her fiction does not explain her neglect by readers today, for James, Howells, Twain and others of her period are widely read, and they treat romantic love hardly more forthrightly than Miss Woolson. It is in matters of intellectual content and style and in scope of theme and treatment of material that James and Howells and Twain excelled her. Moreover, these three managed on occasion to achieve the universal through the use of particular experience and the alembic of the imagination, while most of Miss Woolson's work, as Cowie has observed, lacks "that subtle process of artistic enlargement by which a work passes out of the specific into the universal" (576).

II *Miss Woolson's Contribution to American Fiction*

Despite these shortcomings, Miss Woolson's fiction possesses important historical significance and intrinsic literary values that are worthy of attention today. Kern has clearly demonstrated that she was a pioneer in the local-color movement in the 1870's. He has been less explicit about her contributions to the development of the novel of analysis and to fiction dealing with the so-called international theme in the 1880's and 1890's, but her work in these areas has been acknowledged by others. Indeed, her work in each of these approaches to fiction can hardly be ignored by the literary historian, and scholars have therefore given her attention when the reading public has not.

Miss Woolson's local-color fiction has received more notice recently than anything else she wrote. The very arrangement of Kern's book, for example, lends substance to the casual reader's conclusion that she was primarily a local colorist, for Kern has quite reasonably chosen to deal with her work in relation to the regions in which she lived and about which she wrote. Though this organization is on the whole the most logical one for his purposes, it does tend to obscure her contribution to other currents in the development of fiction. Since the publication of Kern's work in 1934, scholars have stressed her part in the local-color movement. Pattee, Brooks, and Hubbell have been chiefly interested in her stories and novels dealing with the South, and in two recent collections of local-color stories, Constance Woolson's work has been noted and represented. In the earliest of these, *American Local-Color Stories* (1941), Harry R. Warfel and G. Harrison Orians, the editors, have chosen "Solomon" (1873), "Peter the Parson" (1874), and "King David" (1878) to illustrate her interest in Ohio, the Great Lakes country, and the South, respectively. More recently, in *The Local Colorists: American Short Stories, 1857-1900* (1960), Claude M. Simpson has selected "The Lady of Little Fishing" (1874) to represent her handling of lake-country scenes and characters. Thus it is not strange that many of those who know Miss Woolson's work at all know her as a local colorist.

Although there has been a tendency lately to overemphasize her local-color offerings, some scholars have pointed out Miss Woolson's other contributions to the development of fiction in the late nineteenth century. Quinn and Richardson are particularly effective, for example, in dealing with her treatment of Americans in Europe—her efforts along the line of the international theme that intrigued James, Howells, and F. Marion Crawford. And Pattee, Cowie, and Wagenknecht, among others, have discussed her work on the novel of analysis.

In addition to these contributions, Miss Woolson's literary output is also worthy of notice today because she has dealt intelligently and capably with themes and characters of general interest in a technique that is inferior to that of few other American writers of fiction in her day. In regard to theme, for instance, she was one of the first, as Kern has pointed out, to treat small-town life realistically. Far Edgerley in *For the Major* (1883) is not described in the manner of E. W. Howe or Mark Twain—both of whom published novels dealing with life in small towns about this time—but its qualities and the foibles of its characters are brought out no less clearly than those of Twin Mounds in *The Story of a Country Town* (1883) or of St. Petersburg (among others) in *Huckleberry Finn* (1884); and the characterization of its atmosphere is no less memorable.

Constance Woolson has also created a number of vivid and fascinating characters. Her short stories offer Peter the Parson, a high-church Anglican priest who seeks, all too unsuccessfully at first, to serve his Lord among the illiterate folk of a mining settlement in the far north of the Great Lakes country; old Jacques, the Emperor's faithful grenadier despite the passage of many years and many miles since the glorious days of the Empire; Miss Elisabetha, a self-denying but proper spinster from New York who, despite her motherly concern for her protégé (the son of the one man she had loved), loses the boy to an indolent Florida Minorcan girl; "Miss Grief," the American artist in Europe; Prudence Wilkin, the personification of New England duty and self-sacrifice in Old World surroundings; and little Maso, an American boy whose courage and character manifest themselves under difficult conditions in Italy.

In the novels appear Anne Douglas, Madam Carroll, Eve Bruce, Horace Chase—and Margaret Harold, surely Miss Woolson's most arresting creation among her major characters. Critics from James to Cowie have remarked on Margaret's quality, and none with more insight than James himself. Her "great sacrifice"—she rejects, one may recall, the man she loves in order to remain the wife of an unfaithful husband who has repudiated and mistreated her—James terms an "immolation," but it is the author's handling of this aspect of Margaret's character that calls forth the critic's admiration. "The problem," he points out, "was a very interesting one, and worthy to challenge a superior talent—that of making real and natural a transcendent, exceptional act, representing a case in which the sense of duty is raised to exaltation."

Then James follows with an observation that is basic to a just appreciation of many of Miss Woolson's principal characters. "The care, the ingenuity, the precautions the author has exhibited, to make us accept Mrs. Harold in her integrity, are perceptible on every page, and they leave us finally no alternative but to accept her; she remains exalted, but she remains at the same time thoroughly sound. . . . She has drawn Margaret with so close and firm and living a line that she seems to put us in a quandary, if we repudiate her, of denying that a woman *may* look at life from a high point of view" (189-90). And this, of course, is the heart of the matter.

Concerning technique, Miss Woolson's work may, as has been noted, appear dated to twentieth-century readers. When one considers her handling of technique in the perspective of her own time, her fiction bears up well. Aside from James, Howells, and Twain, few Americans writing fiction in the period 1870-94 were her peers. Bret Harte, George W. Cable, and Sarah Orne Jewett come immediately to mind, but the company is small and select. Her art was carefully wrought and sometimes painfully brought to fruition. She was well aware of the latest currents in fiction both in this country and in Europe, and she had read widely in the fiction of the earlier part of the nineteenth century. In the *Times of Melville and Whitman* (1947), Van Wyck Brooks has recently summed up her contributions in theme, character, and technique: "Miss Woolson was a highly conscious writer, careful, skilful, subtle, with a sensitive, clairvoyant feeling for human nature, with the gift of discriminating observation that characterized Howells and Henry James and the talent for analysis that was also appearing in New England" (349).

Many modern critics—Kern and Richardson among them—feel that Miss Woolson's best work was done in her short fiction. Although there is merit in this view, for her short stories and sketches are undeniably good, it robs her total contribution of some of its real significance. Any artist who has written work of the quality of *For the Major, East Angels,* and *Horace Chase*—to say nothing of parts of *Anne* and *Jupiter Lights*—need not be classified chiefly as a writer of tales. Indeed, in her own day, she was considered by some astute critics—namely James, Howells, and Stedman—to be primarily a novelist, and though time has not dealt kindly with some aspects of her novels, *East Angels* and *Horace Chase* remain as examples of her sensitive and delicate artistry worthy of our attention today. Her one novelette, *For the Major,* is a minor classic—as a number of discerning readers have acknowledged.[5] She was not able, it is true, to make the advance that James had hoped for, after *East Angels* (1886), and her limitations are rather obvious to any modern student of fiction; but when one considers the literary balance sheet and sets down against her imperfections the quality of her work in the novel, the excellence of her "short tales" (to use James's term), and the insight expressed in her criticism of fiction, one is still impressed by the overall quality and integrity of her production. One is left to conclude with Cowie that Constance Woolson was indeed a "superior minor writer" and that her books have fallen into undeserved neglect.

That a careful reading of her novels and stories will inform those who wish to know something about the development of fiction in the late nineteenth century has already been demonstrated by Kern, Quinn, Richardson, Cowie, and others. That her work still retains intrinsic literary values of its own remains for a new generation of American readers to discover.

One can only hope that these readers will give Miss Woolson an opportunity to contribute to the twentieth century what she offered in her best work to her own day—a sympathetic understanding and treatment of American character in authentic surroundings by an American artist whose vision was broad enough and whose insight deep enough to include not only her own country but Europe as well. This was her contribution then; it would not be an unworthy contribution now.

Notes and References

Chapter One

1. See especially Fred L. Pattee, "Constance Fenimore Woolson and the South," *South Atlantic Quarterly,* XXXVIII (April, 1939), 130-41 and Lyon N. Richardson, "Constance Fenimore Woolson, 'Novelist Laureate' of America," *South Atlantic Quarterly,* XXXIX (January, 1940), 18-36. Miss Benedict's own work in three volumes is entitled *Five Generations* and was privately printed in London in 1930. The separate volumes—entitled *Voices out of the Past, Constance Fenimore Woolson,* and *The Benedicts Abroad*—are cited hereafter as Benedict, I, II, or III. The second volume contains excerpts from Miss Woolson's letters to friends and relatives, extracts from her notebooks, and selections from her work. It was reprinted with additions in 1932. All references are to the 1930 edition unless otherwise specified.

2. Though Miss Woolson's birthday was variously given in the nineteenth century as having occurred in 1838 or 1848, her good friend, Edmund Clarence Stedman, cited the 1840 date in his biographical sketch in *An American Anthology, 1787-1900* (Boston, 1900), p. 834; and John D. Kern has clearly established that she was born in 1840 (see p. 4).

3. For other details pertaining to Mr. and Mrs. Woolson, see Benedict, I, 94-111, 119-255; Kern, pp. 3-4; and Richardson, pp. 20-23.

4. For an account of this tragedy, see the letter written by Mrs. Clara Woolson Benedict (Constance Woolson's younger sister) to Miss May Harris in 1915: "*In three weeks* of scarlet fever, died No. 3, Anne Cooper Woolson, No. 4, Gertrude Elisabeth Woolson, and No. 5, Julia Campbell Woolson—and Mother with the baby, Constance Fenimore Woolson, only a few days old! Mother nearly lost her reason, and poor Father was told to take her away and he literally lifted Mother into the carriage and drove on and on" (Benedict, I, 41-42).

5. Harlan Hatcher, *The Western Reserve: The Story of New Connecticut in Ohio* (Indianapolis, 1949), pp. 215-17.

6. To Mr. Fay, from St. Augustine, Florida, February 26 [1875?]. This letter is in the files of Mr. Clifton Waller Barrett, of New York City, who very graciously provided me with a photostatic copy of it and gave me permission to quote from it. The other letters by Miss

Woolson in the possession of Mr. Barrett are cited hereafter as belonging to the Barrett Collection, NYC.

7. See *SAQ*, p. 22. For an excerpt from *The Old Stone House*, see Benedict, I, 305-10.

8. January 21, 1891. This letter and others from Miss Woolson to Samuel Mather are now in the possession of his daughter, Mrs. Robert H. Bishop, Jr., of Chagrin Falls, Ohio. Excerpts from many of these letters have previously been printed by Miss Benedict and Richardson. Part of this particular letter, for example, appears in Benedict, II, 46-47 and is quoted in Kern, p. 6.

9. A description of a trip to Zoar appears in Miss Woolson's first magazine article, "The Happy Valley," *Harper's New Monthly Magazine*, XLI (July, 1870), 282-85. She learned something about her father on these trips, and in 1891 she wrote Samuel Mather: "As I look back now, I see it was the romantic side of my father's nature that was pleased with the little Tuscarawas community; father had so much romance. It had but little to feed upon in Ohio. How often I have thought of him as I have wandered about the old world; how much he would have enjoyed it."

10. These letters are quoted in part in Benedict, II, 39-45 and in part in a manuscript article by Miss Guilford entitled "Notes in Memory of Miss Woolson" which Richardson cites in his essay in *SAQ*. The manuscript is held by the Western Reserve Historical Society in Cleveland, and Mrs. Alene Lowe White, the Librarian, has been good enough to send me a copy of it and to allow me to quote from it.

11. Years later, on December 10, 1876, she wrote Daniel C. Eaton, a member of the faculty at Yale and one of her correspondents: "Mackinac is the only spot on earth for which I have what is called 'local attachment.' I often dream of its outline . . . and I always think of it when I am sick." This letter and others to Eaton and two to E. C. Stedman are in the Yale University Library.

12. "Fairy Island," *Putnam's Magazine*, n.s. VI (July, 1870), 62-69 and "Mackinac Island," *Appletons' Journal*, IX (March 8, 1873), 321-23.

13. Miss Benedict and others spell this name *Chegary*, but since Miss Woolson always spells it *Chegaray* in her letters, I have adopted her spelling of the name. For a different opinion on the spelling of this name, see Edd Winfield Parks, *Charles Egbert Craddock (Mary Noailles Murfree)*, (Chapel Hill, 1941), pp. 41-42.

14. This is from an undated letter to Miss May Harris which is reprinted in part in Benedict, I, 292n. A fictional account of this trip is given in Miss Woolson's "The Bones of Our Ancestors," *Harper's*, XLVII (September, 1873), 535-41. This sketch has been

reprinted in Benedict, I, 291-304. For a thinly disguised account of her experience at Madame Chegaray's school, see Miss Woolson's description of Anne Douglas' residence at Madame Moreau's school beginning in Chapter IX of *Anne* (1882).

15. Cooperstown, New York, October 1, 1876. This letter and nineteen others to Stedman are now in various collections in Butler Library, Columbia University. Unless otherwise specified, the letters to Stedman referred to hereafter are those at Butler Library.

Over a year earlier (July 23, 1875) she had written Paul Hamilton Hayne: "What days they were! After all, we *lived* then. It is in vain for our generation to hope to be any other than 'people who remember.' Sometimes even now, I wake early, and think I hear the distant call of the newsboy far down the street, 'Extra! Extra! All about the last battle!'—And then how we rushed out to get it, how we devoured it, and hurried down to the 'Soldiers' Aid' rooms to do the little that was open to us faraway ones to do—prepare boxes of supplies for the soldiers." This letter and twelve others to Hayne are in the Hayne Papers in the Duke University Library. Two of these are quoted in full and others in part in Jay B. Hubbell, "Some New Letters of Constance Fenimore Woolson," *New England Quarterly,* XIV (December, 1941), 715-35.

16. Quoted in the Guilford MS at the Western Reserve Historical Society. Much of this information may also be found in a letter of the same time to Mrs. Samuel Mather (Benedict, II, 362).

17. See the *Book Buyer,* VI (October, 1889), 309-11. Though Stedman, the son of E. C. Stedman, had received some of his information from Miss Woolson herself, Kern was never able to locate the anonymous contributions mentioned in the essay, and he concluded that there was "no evidence of any contributions to religious magazines before 1870" (p. 6n).

18. See Benedict, I, 108-11 and Kern, p. 7. For Constance Woolson's own sketch of her father's life, see Benedict, I, 94-101.

19. See Kern, pp. 46-47, 180-81. Miss Woolson later wrote Mrs. Harriet Benedict Sherman that George A. Benedict's "encouragement and interest were everything" to her when she began to write. And, she continued, "I don't believe I should have gone on if I had not had them behind me just at that time. He was always very kind to me, and in just the way I needed. I was so despondent, and the future looked so dark, yet I wouldn't betray how I felt. They were hard years for me, and your father was my mainstay" (Benedict, II, 29-30).

20. For the difficulties involved (the paucity of records chiefly) in making an accurate account of Miss Woolson's activities in the 1870's (and much the same thing on a lesser scale may be said of the years in Europe, 1879-94), see Kern, p. 46. Richardson's essay,

though brief, has contributed some information on this matter and many of Miss Woolson's unpublished letters throw some light on it, but a full treatment is still not possible in the 1960's.

21. Benedict, I, 230-31. For other impressions of St. Augustine, see Miss Woolson's long two-part travel article called "The Ancient City" in the issues of *Harper's* for December, 1874, and January, 1875.

22. See Laura Stedman and George M. Gould, *Life and Letters of Edmund Clarence Stedman* (New York, 1910), I, 504. This work is hereafter cited as Stedman and Gould.

23. The manuscripts of the first and third letters referred to are in Butler Library, Columbia University. The first and second letters are quoted in part in Stedman and Gould, I, 521-22 and II, 320.

In an undated letter (obviously written in the last half of the 1870's) to her cousin, George Pomeroy Keese, Miss Woolson refers to Stedman: "He knows all the literary people, ladies as well as men, and takes an interest in them that is so real and generous and above anything like small jealousy, that they all like him. I only know him in a 'literary' way. But in that way we are great friends. I met him first in Florida, when I was scarcely known at all as a beginner at writing even; and he immediately took the kindest interest in all I was doing, or rather, attempting to do. He is the most loyal of friends, as well as a very outspoken one, at least so he seemed to me" (Benedict, II, 30).

24. Her aunt's sincere regard for the state led Miss Benedict to establish the Constance Fenimore Woolson Memorial House at Rollins College, Winter Park, Florida. Since the dedication of Woolson House on May 31, 1938, a little pamphlet entitled "A Catalogue of Memorabilia Relating to Constance Fenimore Woolson" has appeared and may be obtained from Rollins College.

25. Hayne Papers, Duke University Library. Quoted in Hubbell's article in the *NEQ*, p. 727.

26. Hayne Papers, Duke University Library. Printed in part in Hubbell, p. 722.

27. Hayne Papers, Duke University Library. Quoted in Hubbell, p. 731.

28. On April 16, 1876, she observed in a letter to Hayne: "Don't you think that for a red hot abolitionist, Republican, and hard-money advocate, I have behaved well down here in Dixie during these last three long years? I think I ought to have a word of commendation when you consider that the pen has been in my hands all the time, and that the beaten track was all the other way. I have tried to 'put myself in their place,' and at least be fair." Also quoted in Hubbell, p. 731.

29. That she had no intention of expatriating herself permanently is quite clear from the number of references in her letters to her

plans for returning home and to her intense patriotism. Something of her feeling along these lines may be observed in a hitherto unpublished letter she wrote Hamilton W. Mabie, an editor of the *Christian Union* in the 1880's, on June 18, 1883, three and a half years after she had gone to Europe: "Our 'country,' and all that means—patriotism in its warmest form, was burned into us by a red-hot fire, and the results are ineffaceable. And so though I should stay years over here, I remain as I was when I first landed. . . ." This letter is also at the Duke University Library, and I am grateful to my wife, Margaret Bear Moore, who found the letter tucked away in the Library's copy of *For the Major*, for relinquishing to me her right to publication.

30. For the remarks cited in this paragraph, see the letters quoted in Benedict, II, 48, 152-59. The article on Mentone (January and February, 1884), together with others in *Harper's* on Cairo (October and November, 1891) and Corfu (August, 1892), later formed the basis (with some additional material) for the posthumously published *Mentone, Cairo, and Corfu* (1896).

31. Since few of the many letters exchanged between James and Miss Woolson are extant today, the chief evidence for their friendship lies in the excerpts from various letters printed in Benedict II and III, though these leave much to be inferred. Mrs. Benedict, for example, once wrote a friend: "Henry James was an intimate friend of my sister's; he and she both being talented writers formed a friendship that never failed—and when my sister died suddenly in Venice, Henry took my daughter and myself into a very close friendship on her account" (Benedict, III, 2n). There are also several remarks that Miss Woolson made in letters to Samuel Mather that Miss Benedict did not print. There is this passage, for instance, in a letter of April 29, 1893: "You will see that in all this [she plans to leave England for Italy], I am giving up the being near my kind friend, Mr. James. I don't know what made me tell you . . . [about] that last message of his sister to me—that touched me so much. But I suppose it was simply the relief of having some of my own family to talk to, after being so long alone. I felt that I could say anything to you, without having to think whether it was safe or not, wise or not, prudent or not.—But Mr. J. will come to Italy every year, and perhaps we can write that play after all."

The letters and telegrams (Miss Guilford remarks in her manuscript article that James "used often to send [Miss Woolson] sprightly telegraph messages in substitute for talk") exchanged between the two are hard to come by now. Miss Clare Benedict wrote me from Lucerne on November 24, 1960, that their correspondence "was destroyed by them as soon as letters were answered." There are, however, four of Miss Woolson's letters written to James in the 1880's at Houghton Library, Harvard University. Since these letters are restricted to the use of someone else, I have not been able to examine them. Other letters may also have escaped burning, but if so, they are not available today.

32. This was very important to her. On February 24, 1887, she wrote Stedman about her new home: "After seventeen years of wandering, I have at last a home of my own—(though but a temporary one). Such joy as I take in my own tables & chairs, tea-cups & cushions, I don't believe you can imagine; but Mrs. Stedman can." After explaining the economy of this manner of living in Italy, she continued: "But the view, & the air, & the scene, & the flowers, & the sense of ownership (for a year)—the tranquility of spirit, the far-awayness—these to me, just now, seem infinite riches."

33. This letter and fourteen others to Fiske, the former librarian and professor of North-European languages at Cornell University who had retired from the faculty in 1883 and removed to Florence where he came to know Miss Woolson and to be her neighbor at the Villa Forini, are at the Cornell University Library.

34. In an article in *Harper's Weekly* for February 3, 1894 (written before the circumstances of her death were known), Henry Mills Alden, editor of *Harper's New Monthly* and a long-time friend of Miss Woolson's, quoted from several letters written in the last months of her life (one on "New-Year's day," 1894). But he cites these in such a way as to make it difficult for one to be sure that what he is quoting belongs to a particular date. After referring to a "letter to an old friend [possibly Alden himself], written last New-Year's day," he paraphrases part of the letter, then discourses for some lines on her capacity as a writer and the reaction of the critics and reading public to her work, and finally suggests that "in the despondency of those last days at Venice she underrated her past achievement." Then he quotes Miss Woolson, but one cannot be sure that the passage is from the letter of January 1: " 'I have given up my broken sword to Fate, the Conqueror,' she writes, quoting Thackeray. Again: 'I am finishing up the fringes and edges of my literary work, for I feel that I shall do very little more. Or course, this feeling may change. But at present it has full possession of me; I am profoundly discouraged.' " A few lines later, Alden quotes her again, but he says nothing about the source. " 'If I could go into a convent,' she writes, '(where I didn't have to confess, nor rise before daylight for icy matins), I think I could write three or four novels better than any I have yet done. But there are no worldly convents. So I'll write my new effusions on another star, and send them back to you by telepathy' " (113). It is quite possible, of course, that all the above quotations are from one letter written on January 1, 1894, but one cannot positively assert

that such is the case. One may, however, reasonably infer that these lines were written in the last months of Miss Woolson's life and that they provide further evidence of the presence of her "deadly enemy."

35. For the details surrounding Miss Woolson's death, see Kern, pp. 159-62; Miss Guilford's MS "Notes in Memory of Miss Woolson"; Richardson's article, p. 21; and the various newspaper and magazine accounts cited in Kern's bibliography, especially the articles in *Harper's Weekly* for February 3 and 10, 1894.

The cables from Europe to Samuel Mather about his aunt's death are with her letters to him in the papers now in the possession of Mrs. Robert H. Bishop, Jr. One of these is especially interesting. Grace Carter, a relative and devoted friend, went to the Casa Semitecolo shortly after Miss Woolson's death and cabled Mather on January 27, 1894, as follows: "Aunt Constance [Mrs. Carter was actually a cousin] had influenza night nurse left her for moment for something needed in sudden delirium fell from window to street. Picked up immediately lived short time unconscious with no apparent pain face looked very peaceful no will found."

In her last letter to Mather (December 20-21, 1893), Miss Woolson mentioned that she was making a new will, but since she had written him about her various wills as early as January 21, 1891, and since he handled many of her business affairs, her statement does not seem unusual.

36. On this matter, see Miss Woolson's letter of December 10, 1880, to Miss Mather in Benedict, II, 237-38. "Yes, I meet quite a good many people I know, and I have made a number of new acquaintances. But I am, after all, a solitary sort of an old bird, and, as poor Sothern used to say, 'flock by myself.' I am all the time busy, and I am not strong enough to take much part in society, or to go out much, and do writing-work at the same time. The best of me goes into my writing, and so, on the whole, I prefer to write quietly for the freshest part of the day, take a good walk, and then curl up in an easy-chair with an entertaining book, and go to bed early. If people will be so kind as to seek me out in my leisure time, or come and go to walk with me, I am delighted; but that is all the time I have for them!"

Three years earlier she had written to Stedman on September 16, 1877: "But do you not know how strong a feeling I have about making new acquaintances? I would go twenty miles any day to avoid it. It was always somewhat so with me; it is now much increased. I have not, *personally*, a particle of self-confidence. Persons have to like me, and show they like me, before I can get up my courage to talk naturally to them. Now who is going to take this trouble for a woman like me? Hardly anyone. I know this, and no longer expect it; or place myself where I look as though I expected it."

And, even earlier, on July 23, 1875, she had confided to Hayne: "For, Mr. Hayne, if there is anything I dread it is a new acquaintance. I evade, and avoid, and back away from everybody. It is, unfortunately, my nature to do so. I am sorry. It is a great fault. But I cannot change it now, I fear, after so many years' indulgence."

One suspects that, apart from a natural shyness and a discriminating taste in people as well as in everything else, Miss Woolson's growing deafness in the 1870's led her gradually to withdraw from others and frequently to shun social gatherings. Even though these were her sentiments on the matter, she did not eschew society altogether. Years later in Europe she took great pleasure in the company of friends in Florence, Venice, and Oxford.

37. For Miss Benedict's comments, see II, ix-xii. I am aware, of course, that Miss Benedict is a prejudiced interpreter in such matters, but she also knew her aunt more intimately than any of those who have written about her. Indeed, Miss Woolson herself observed on several occasions that Clare's personality closely resembled her own (III, 12, 39).

Chapter Two

1. Benedict, II (1932), 553. Miss Woolson's juvenile, called *The Old Stone House*, was written under the pseudonym of Anne March. D. Lothrop & Company published it in Boston, 1872.

2. See, for example, "Margaret Morris," *Appletons' Journal*, VII (April 13, 1872), 394-99; "Ballast Island," *Appletons'*, IX (June 28, 1873), 833-39; and "A Flower of the Snow," *The Galaxy*, XVII (January, 1874), 76-85. The first of these concerns a proud young lady from New England who feels contempt for her fellow passengers on a lake steamer. She comes to her senses only after a storm sinks the vessel and she discovers that those whom she had despised have more courage in the face of danger than she has. The account of the sinking of the *Chippewa* is the best part of this piece.

"Ballast Island" contains within its conventional love-story framework one of the most memorable sketches of character in Miss Woolson's early work: Miss Jonah, a North Georgia woman who leaves her home for an island in Lake Erie so that her fiancé may marry her sister. In the treatment of Miss Jonah's character and dialect, this work looks forward to the Southern sketches to come; in the development of the theme of self-sacrifice, it also anticipates the novels.

Like "Ballast Island," "A Flower of the Snow" is a love story; and, like so many of the lake-country sketches, it has a Mackinac setting. Flower Moran, a plain little teacher from New England, falls in love with Lieutenant Maxwell Ruger, a "stalwart young Saxon" at Fort Holmes, who at first takes the romance rather lightly. When, however, Flower, feeling that he does not truly love her, leaves the village with the mail pack, Max follows her in the knowledge that he loves her enough to brave a blinding snowstorm. He catches up with her after both have been almost frozen by the storm, and they are married by Père Ronan, a hermit priest who reminds one of both Père Piret and Père Michaux in other lake-country fiction and whose portrait in this piece may well be a preparatory study for the later characterizations of Piret and Michaux.

3. In a letter of June 15, 1875, to Hayne, Miss Woolson remarks on Howells' review of the book in general and his criticism of "Castle Nowhere" in particular:

> But the criticism, as a whole, was very high praise, I thought; of course I am smarting a little about the 'Castle,' which, to tell the truth, *was* something of an ideal, instead of a *real* tale—like the others. But then I had been abused so for writing such deadly 'real' stories, that I did branch out, in that one, into the realm of the imagination. Still, Mr. Howells is mistaken in thinking that situation fantastic; the islands, the fogs, the false lights, the wreckers, the Mormons are all exactly from real life, true descriptions.

4. VIII (September, 1874), 600-10 and IX (December, 1874), 232-43. "Peter the Parson" has recently been reprinted in *American Local-Color Stories* (1941).

E. C. Stedman apparently persuaded Richard Watson Gilder, one of the editors of *Scribner's*, to publish both stories. Miss Woolson refers to them in a letter to Stedman of April 13, 1874: "I shall be ever so glad if you can stir up Mr. Gilder to publish 'Jeannette.' Not that it is a good story; but it is weary waiting for a first appearance." A few lines later, she points out that the editors "don't like" "Peter the Parson" and concludes: ". . . in my opinion it is the most powerful thing I have ever written." This letter and another of October 10, 1876, are in the Yale University Library.

5. Miss Woolson was criticized for allowing the minister to be killed in the story. Her reaction was expressed in a letter of April 25 [1875?] to Samuel Mather: "Under the abuse which has been showered upon me for my 'brutal' killing of 'Peter the Parson,' I have steadily maintained to myself that both in an artistic and truthful-to-life point of view, my ending of the story was better than the conversion of the miners, the plenty to eat, and the happy marriage proposed by my critics." Part of this letter has been printed in Benedict, II, 23.

6. Despite her modest reference to "Jeannette" in her letter to Stedman, Miss Woolson liked the story, as she wrote James R. Osgood, because it was "such an accurate picture of Mackinac" (Kern, p. 25).

7. "St. Clair Flats" has been reprinted in Benedict, II (1932), 431-57.

8. "Solomon," XXXII (October, 1873), 413-24; "Wilhelmina," XXXV (January, 1875), 44-55; and "The Lady of Little Fishing," XXXV (September, 1874), 293-305. The first of these has been reprinted in *American Local-Color Stories* (1941), pp. 188-206; the last, in *The Local Colorists: American Short Stories, 1857-1900* (1960), pp. 130-51.

9. *The Local Colorists,* p. 130. For other views of "Solomon" and "Wilhelmina," see p. 129 and Kern, pp. 33-34.

10. Among the other sketches that might have been included in this collection, two should be mentioned: "Crowder's Cove: A Story of the War," *Appletons'*, XV (March 18,1876), 357-62, and "Black Point," *Harper's,* LIX (June, 1879), 84-97. "Crowder's Cove" appeared more than two years before Mary Murfree's first tale of the Tennessee mountains came out in the *Atlantic* in May, 1878. John Crowder is a relatively prosperous Southern mountaineer who remains "neutral" in the Civil War. The two leading female characters—one from the North and the other from the South—are "outlanders." The point of the story is the contrast drawn between Southern ways as represented by Sally Trellington and Northern ways as represented by Elinor Kent. In the climax of the contest that ensues, Sally wins out, but there is honor for both young ladies and for both sides. "Black Point," by way of contrast, has a Florida setting; but it is chiefly memorable because Lola Valdez foreshadows the lovely, indolent, irresponsible Garda Thorne in *East Angels,* and Eleanor Fordyce and Pierre Brandon bear more than a slight resemblance to Margaret Harold and Evert Winthrop in the same novel. The theme of self-sacrifice and renunciation is also sounded in both works, but in the sketch Brandon wins Eleanor despite her willingness to sacrifice herself for him.

11. Kern suggests that Andersonville, Georgia, is the actual scene of this story.

On several occasions in her letters, Miss Woolson remarked on her feeling for cemeteries where soldiers were buried. She wrote Hayne on September 12, 1875: "I always go to see the soldiers' graves. I cannot bear to think that they are so soon forgotten; as they *are,* at the North—and indeed the War itself is already a thing of the past up there."

12. *The South in American Literature, 1607-1900* (Durham, 1954), p. 737. This work is cited hereafter as *SAL.*

An interesting change was made in the magazine text when Miss Woolson revised it for publication in book form. The following passage, for obvious reasons, was deleted from the revised text:

> [BETTINA WARD:] 'Grief covers our land.'
> [RODMAN:] 'Yes, for a mighty wrong brings ever in its train a mighty sorrow.'
> Miss Ward turned upon him fiercely. 'Do you, who have lived among us, dare to pretend that the state of our servants is not worse this moment than it ever was before?'
> 'Transition.'
> 'A horrible transition!'
> 'Horrible, but inevitable; education will be the savior. Had I fifty millions to spend on the South tomorrow, every cent should go for schools, and for schools alone.'
> 'For the negroes, I suppose,' said the girl with bitter scorn.
> 'For the negroes, and for the whites also,' answered John Rodman gravely. 'The lack of general education is painfully apparent everywhere throughout the South; it is from that cause more than any other that your beautiful country now lies desolate.'
> 'Desolate—desolate indeed,' said Miss Ward [*Atlantic*, XXXIX, 276].

This bit of editorial work, among other things, suggests, as Kern has pointed out, that "Miss Woolson thoroughly understood the bitterness that was in the hearts of the southern people during that period when short-sighted northern statesmanship was rubbing salt into the old wounds. She knew the facts and she had the artistry to dramatize them. No student of American history during this troubled era can afford to neglect this and the other stories of hers which reveal so poignantly the effects of the war and of Reconstruction on individual southerners" (74).

The text of "Rodman" in book form has been reprinted in Benedict, II (1932), 468-94.

13. *American Fiction* (New York, 1936), p. 334. Kern describes "Sister St. Luke" as "one of the finest stories" of the Florida group of Southern tales (61). For an unfavorable view of the work, based chiefly on the implausibility of Sister St. Luke's heroic action in the storm, see Thomas Sergeant Perry, "Some Recent Novels," *Atlantic*, XLVI (July, 1880), 125.

When the story appeared in book form, John Hay wrote an epigraph for it (42). See also the *Complete Poetical Works of John Hay* (Boston, 1916), p. 74.

14. *Appletons'*, XIII (March 13, 1875), 327-34. This sketch has been reprinted in Lyon N. Richardson and others, eds., *The Heritage of American Literature* (Boston, 1951), II, 252-64.

15. In her letters Miss Woolson often comments on marriage and family life. She wrote Samuel Mather, for example, on January 21,

1891, regarding the meaning of family life to a spinster: "All the same it's the best thing in life; it's the only thing worth living for; this is the sincere belief—& the result of the observations—of one who has never had it!"

16. *Harper's,* LII (April, 1876), 662-74. "Old Gardiston" has recently been reprinted in Milton L. Ellis and others, eds., *The College Book of American Literature* (New York, 1940), II, 587-602.

T. S. Perry did not like this tale any more than he had liked "Sister St. Luke" (see above, note 13). His discussion of "Old Gardiston" in the *Atlantic* is an excellent example of the type of sectional bias one finds frequently expressed in the Boston magazine's pages at the time:

> The cantrips of Miss Gardis Duke . . . read like what one finds oftener in poor novels than in real life. This young person, Miss Duke, is a little chit, who, in extreme poverty, imitates the splendors of her former opulence, and gives the rough edge of her saucy tongue to two of her lovers, Union officers, who just after the late war are stationed near her house. She invites them to dinner, and then, when they are gone, she burns up the shabby finery in which she received them. . . . Certainly, this little cat is not a very impressive person, and it is not easy to interest one's self in such a lump of affectation; but Miss Woolson seems to take her at her own pompous valuation, and to see heroism in her imitation of tawdry novels. Finally, she steps down from her pinnacle of conceit, and marries one of the officers, and we have no doubt that by this time she has satisfactorily taken vengeance for everything that happened during the war.

17. In a letter of July 23, 1876, to Stedman, Miss Woolson took up the matter of "love-making" in this story: "Why did you find fault with the love-making in 'Old Gardiston,' I wonder: such a small bit of it there was too! I always steer clear of it if possible; I am afraid of betraying my ignorance. . . ."

18. For other evidence of Miss Woolson's respect for the South Carolina character, see her letter of July 23, 1875, to Hayne and her contribution on old-fashioned South Carolina gentlemen in the *Atlantic,* XLII (August, 1878), 245-47. Part of the letter to Hayne is quoted in Hubbell's "Some New Letters of CFW," 722.

19. See "Culture and Progress," *Scribner's,* XX (August, 1880), 633-34, and the "Editor's Study," *Harper's,* LXXIV (February, 1887), 482. "The South Devil" first appeared in the *Atlantic,* XLV (February, 1880), 173-93, and is Miss Woolson's most recent publication in the collection, though it had been written in 1877.

20. For an interesting parallel and possible source of the account

of Ralph Kinsolving's death in the North as a Confederate spy, see Miss Woolson's own travel sketch, "The Wine Islands of Lake Erie," in *Harper's*, XLVII (June, 1873), 27-36. There, among other things, she describes the efforts of John Yates Beall, a young Virginia officer, to release the Confederate prisoners on Johnson's Island by attacking the Sandusky Bay area from the lake side. The account closes with Beall's capture, trial, conviction, and subsequent execution as a spy in the North.

21. Kern reaches a different conclusion. "It is doubtful," he points out, "whether Miss Woolson succeeds in making credible the self-effacement of 'Bro.' Characters of such nobility . . . may exist in this world, but we expect writers of good fiction to be guided by probability rather than possibility. Beyond a certain point idealism easily becomes sentimentalism, and in this story the writer over-steps the bounds of reality and enters the land of unalloyed romance. Delighting as she always does in pointing out the evidences of unselfishness in characters who are otherwise commonplace, Miss Woolson in this tale puts entirely too much strain on the credulity of the reader" (69-70).

22. *Scribner's*, XV (April, 1878), 781-89. "King David" has been reprinted in *American Local-Color Stories*, pp. 225-41.

23. Miss Woolson makes a similar point about another New Englander in "Jeannette" (see chapter II above). In an aside on Rodney Prescott's concern about the possibility of the "taint" of "negro blood" in Jeannette, the narrator remarks: "Theoretically he believed in the equality of the enslaved race, and stood ready to maintain the belief with his life, but practically he held himself entirely aloof from them; the Southern creed and practice were the exact reverse" (167).

24. In regard to Southern literary taste, see also Miss Woolson's letter of August 21, 1874, to Stedman and scattered comments in *East Angels* (especially 31, 150-51).

25. This letter is in the Barrett Collection, NYC.

26. James's choice of diction in 1887 may be a bit misleading. His reference to the "*voicelessness* of the conquered and reconstructed South" may be appropriate to the 1870's when most of the stories in *Rodman* first appeared in print, but it is far less proper to describe the 1880's when Southern work appeared frequently in the major Northern literary magazines. For the most part, however, James has shrewdly evaluated Miss Woolson's work in this vein.

27. Pattee thought well of these stories. In the *Cambridge History of American Literature*, he remarked: "And still later in Italy she caught again the soul of a people and wrought it into the tales to be collected under the title *The Front Yard*" (II, 382).

One is curious to know why "'Miss Grief'," the first story that Miss Woolson wrote after she went abroad and an excellent piece of work, was not included in this collection or in *Dorothy*. The one or two points of similarity between this tale and "The Street of the Hyacinth" should hardly have prevented the publishers from including both in the same collection.

In "'Miss Grief'," the central character Aaronna Crief (Moncrief, one learns later) goes to Rome to get some advice on her literary work from a fellow American who has had some financial success as an author in Europe. The story is narrated by this writer, who, impressed with Miss Moncrief's work, tries to sell it to some of his literary connections. He even tries to edit the work, a drama of great power, but he finds that it cannot be easily changed without the destruction of its individuality. The publishers reject the play, but, when the narrator finds "Miss Grief" dying, he lies to her about the rejection of the manuscript; and she dies contented in the knowledge that her work will be brought out. There are several points of resemblance between the narrator and Henry James: both are men who have inherited money and know the "way of society"; both model their work a "little on Balzac"; both are interested in psychological motivation of character in their fiction; and both use the term "the figure in the carpet" in similar ways. A comparison of this story with "The Street of the Hyacinth" appears in Chapter IV below.

"'Miss Grief'" appeared first in *Lippincott's*, XXV (May, 1880), 574-85, and was later reprinted in *Stories by American Authors*, IV, New York, 1884, 5-39.

28. In a letter of March 2, 1882, Miss Woolson described her visit to Paestum: "Here [Salerno] we . . . started on our grand day's excursion to Paestum, to see the Greek Temples—the one thing in Italy, south of Rome, in which I have felt the deepest interest. . . . After a while, the great columns of the temples began to loom up against the blue. We . . . drove directly to the ruins. But 'ruins' they can hardly be called, so perfectly are they preserved. . . . I was not in the least disappointed in my first sight of Greek columns; indeed, the Temple of Neptune seemed to me the most perfect building I have ever seen. . . . I mean, in pure simple beauty" (Benedict, II, 264-65).

29. A reviewer in the *Critic* thought "In Venice" the "best piece of work, besides the first story" in the volume.

30. A few verbal and stylistic changes have been made by the publishers in several of the stories, but they are of little importance in comparison with those made by Miss Woolson herself in preparing some of her earlier pieces for publication in *Castle Nowhere* and in *Rodman the Keeper*.

31. Though the date 1896 appears on the title page of the book, is was copyrighted in 1895. As was the custom in the publishing business at this time, *Dorothy* was brought out in time for the Christmas trade in 1895.

32. The five pieces comprising *Dorothy* appeared in the following order in the magazines: "A Florentine Experiment," *Atlantic,* XLVI (October, 1880), 502-30; "At the Château of Corinne," *Harper's* LXXV (October, 1887), 778-96; "Dorothy," *Harper's, LXXXIV* (March, 1892), 551-75; "A Transplanted Boy," *Harper's,* LXXXVIII (February, 1894), 425-41; and "A Waitress," *Harper's,* LXXXIX (June, 1894), 88-102.

33. This letter is in the possession of Mrs. Robert H. Bishop, Jr., Chagrin Falls, Ohio. The passage has been previously quoted in Benedict, II, 192. Miss Woolson also refers to James and to their visits to the galleries in several other letters of this period printed in part in Benedict, II, 185-92.

34. "I am fascinated," Miss Woolson wrote Samuel Mather from Geneva in October of 1880, with "the 'eighteenth-century' people" who lived on "the shores of this lake": ". . . I feel as if I had been the intimate friend of Mesdames Recamier and de Stael, and of all those witty people of that letter-writing day."

35. Constance Woolson had earlier expressed herself on this matter in a letter of July 23, 1876, to E. C. Stedman. Concerning her friend's "entire disbelief in the possibility of true fiery genius in woman," she remarks: "Well—I do not quarrel with you about this; and the reason is—that I fully agree with you!"

36. Interestingly enough, this story had been kept by the editors of *Harper's* for "seven or eight years" before it was published. Miss Woolson wrote Mrs. Samuel Mather that she "had forgotten all about it, and re-read it to see what was in it" (Benedict, II, 47).

37. The story apparently had some influence on the sale of the song in question—"Through the Long Days"—for Miss Woolson wrote Samuel Mather from Oxford on October 14, 1892, seven months after "Dorothy" had appeared in *Harper's,* that Mr. Boott had told her that the clerks at Ditson's (the Boston music publisher) had been "astonished by the call for 'that old song' . . ., which had been reposing undisturbed on their shelves for years" (Benedict, II, 45-46).

38. Miss Benedict lists it, together with "Rodman the Keeper" and "Old Gardiston," as "favourites" among the short stories mentioned in the letters she received in response to the publication of *Five Generations* in the 1930's. See *Appreciations of Voices Out of the Past, Constance Fenimore Woolson, The Benedicts Abroad: The Family Trilogy* (Leatherhead, Surrey, 1941), p. x.

39. Leigh North, in the *New York Times Saturday Review,* quoted in Benedict, II (1932), 556.

40. Either " 'Miss Grief' " (*Lippincott's,* May, 1880) or "In Sloane Street" (*Harper's Bazar,* June 11, 1892) might have been included, for they are both better stories than this one.

41. "Comment on New Books," LXXVII (January, 1896), 129. Though these comments are made in regard to *The Front Yard,* the writer concludes by noting that they are also applicable to *Dorothy.*

Chapter Three

1. When Miss Woolson was still writing *Anne,* James R. Osgood apparently approached her about publishing it. She wrote Stedman on September 16, 1877, that "Mr. Osgood will take it if I please. But I want to have it pushed a little." The following May she informed Stedman that the work was finished, but it did not appear in that year. Early in 1879 she broached the subject to Stedman again: "Do you wonder what has become of my novel? I think you will see it in print during the year. I say no more; although I *would like to.* You can have no idea how fond I am now of Mr. Osgood. I fairly dream of him at night." For some reason, Osgood did not bring out the book. Financial difficulties which led him to merge with H. O. Houghton in 1878 may have been responsible for his failure to publish it. At any rate, Harper and Brothers accepted the manuscript and prepared to run it first as a serial in the firm's monthly magazine, but *Anne* encountered another delay before the first installment finally appeared in the December issue of *Harper's* in 1880. In October Miss Woolson wrote Samuel Mather that the novel was being held up because the editors of the magazine wanted to serialize it concurrently in the new English edition of the monthly which was to begin in December, and she concluded: "This—the Ed. of the Magazine—considered quite a feather in my cap; and I could see that he thought the honor to me compensated for all the delay. But as I could not *tell* this, the delay has been, to me, annoying. There is no secret about it now of course."

2. All references to the text of the novel are to the first edition in book form, which Miss Woolson revised from the magazine text. Since it was always her general practice to revise her magazine work carefully before book publication, all references to the novels in this chapter, unless otherwise specified, are to the first editions.

3. William Wallace in *The Academy,* XXIV (July 21, 1883), 42. For other British considerations of Miss Woolson's fiction, see Kern, pp. 193-94.

4. Published first in serial form by *Harper's,* November, 1882,

to April, 1883, *For the Major* was brought out as a book under the Harper imprint in the late spring of 1883.

5. *East Angels* appeared in successive issues of *Harper's* from January, 1885, to May, 1886, and was brought out in book form by the parent firm of Harper and Brothers in 1886.

In a letter of July 28, 1960, Mr. Edwin F. Barber, of Harper and Brothers, the original publishers of all save three of Miss Woolson's books, reported to me the following approximate sales figures:

Anne	57,600
East Angels	10,450
Jupiter Lights	6,000
For the Major	5,750
Horace Chase	5,000
The Front Yard	3,000
Dorothy	2,250
Rodman the Keeper	2,250

These figures do not include the number of copies of *Rodman* sold by D. Appleton, the original publisher of that volume, nor is there any approximate count for *The Old Stone House* or *Castle Nowhere,* both of which were brought out by Boston houses. I am grateful to Mr. Barber for his courtesy in sending these figures to me.

6. *Cavalcade of the American Novel,* p. 174. See also Arthur H. Quinn, *American Fiction*, pp. 338-40 and Alexander Cowie, *The Rise of the American Novel,* pp. 573-74.

7. The Winthrop-Garda Thorne relationship, as well as that between Chase and Ruth Franklin, is to some extent foreshadowed in "Miss Vedder," one of Miss Woolson's uncollected stories from *Harper's* (March, 1879). In "Miss Vedder," for example, Howell Dwight, a forty-one-year-old Northern man of means, falls in love with Fanny Singleton, a beautiful but indolent Southern girl of seventeen whose family has recently moved north. Their romance is abetted by Rachel Vedder, a wealthy cousin of Dwight's in her thirties who has secretly been in love with him for years. When Mrs. Singleton on her deathbed mourns about Fanny's future, Dwight offers to marry her, and they are joined in wedlock on the spot by an Episcopal clergyman who happens to be present.

But Fanny does not love Dwight any more than Garda loves Winthrop or Ruth loves Chase; and inevitably Miss Vedder catches Fanny stealing off to see Robert Strain, her old Southern swain. Rachel brings the romance to an end by financing Strain's departure to parts unknown, and when Fanny dies a few years later, Dwight is still ignorant of her love for another man. Thus Rachel Vedder sacrifices herself for Dwight in much the same way that Margaret

Harold sacrifices herself for Evert Winthrop, though Mrs. Harold is also upholding a principle that is not involved in Miss Vedder's situation.

In the lack of understanding that is revealed in the case of Dwight and Fanny one can readily foresee the whole situation obtaining later between Winthrop and Garda and between Chase and Ruth. Moreover, all three men are quite obtuse about women (and about young women in particular). As Miss Vedder's Aunt Maria puts it, " 'Men are like that about young girls always when they get to be toward forty and a little blasé; they believe any thing.' " Finally, Mrs. Singleton and Mrs. Thorne reveal something in common as they prepare to die. Both think of the future of their respective daughters and manage to extract promises from those present to see to it that they are cared for. Mrs. Franklin in *Horace Chase* has already accomplished this end long before she dies.

8. That Miss Woolson felt she was on solid ground in her characterization of Margaret she makes clear in a letter of August 10, 1889, to Stedman. "As to my Margaret in 'East Angels' . . . , I have known just such a woman; & more than one." This merely means, of course, that Miss Woolson felt she had precedents from life itself to support her interpretation of Margaret. It does not mean that she simply sketched in this instance someone she knew, for her views on this aspect of the relationship between life and fiction had also been expressed in an earlier letter of August 4, 1882, to Stedman. "Real persons," she remarked to her friend, "are seldom usable in a novel."

9. Quoted in Lyon N. Richardson, "Constance Fenimore Woolson, 'Novelist Laureate' of America," p. 31. *Jupiter Lights* appeared in successive issues of *Harper's* from January to September, 1889; it was brought out in book form by the Harper firm in the fall of 1889.

10. Concerning Miss Woolson's interest in the drama, one is not surprised to find that in the 1890's she planned to do a play with Henry James. In a letter written from Oxford on April 29, 1893, she remarked to Samuel Mather: "But Mr. James will come to Italy every year, and perhaps we can write that play after all."

11. Miss Woolson apparently had some difficulty in arriving at a title for the novel since she wrote her nephew on October 14, 1892, that she had sent the Harper firm three or four "possible names" and that J. Henry Harper had suggested "For Better, for Worse" as a title. This was tentatively accepted but changed to "Horace Chase," one of Miss Woolson's own suggestions, just prior to publication in the magazine. For Henry Mills Alden's letter of July 27, 1892, containing Harper's suggested title, see J. Henry Harper, *The House of Harper* (New York, 1912), p. 485.

12. For references to Mather's "advice" and "excellent corrections,"

see Miss Woolson's letter to him of March 14, 1893. In addition to her words of gratitude, she says: "I wish very much that I could have been near you through the whole process of putting this novel together." Had this been the case, one may suppose that Horace Chase would have emerged a full-blown character and that the novel would have benefitted considerably from Mather's knowledge of and experience in the business world.

Chapter Four

1. She was, however, very much aware, as she wrote in her notebook, of "the danger, as one grows older, of clinging to the author of one's youth too much. Of feeling no interest in the newer or younger ones. It is true that most persons—as regards books, music, art—stop when they reach a certain age; you can tell when they left off reading the new, keeping up with the march of the times, by the books, music, etc., they speak of. For instance, I know many who have never gone beyond Dickens and Thackeray."

2. Stedman replied on September 2: "Never tell me again that you are a 'realist.' That word, and 'romancer,' are merely terms." The "realism-romanticism conflict," he continued, "amounts to nothing, except that all 'school' conflicts are stimulating. . . . You are what God made you—a woman of taste, industry, insight, *plus* genius; and *your* so-called realistic method is charged no less with passion and imagination. 'Tis a poor workman who can't use any tool. Forgive this digressional preachment" (Stedman and Gould, II, 140-41).

3. Interestingly enough, Miss Woolson on at least one occasion remarked on the relationship between "real" people and fictional characters. In a letter of August 4, 1882, she inquired of Stedman: "But why do you again accuse me of putting real persons into my pages? Real persons are seldom usable in a novel. They can only serve, I think, as—something of which one says—remember *not* to have it like so-&-so."

4. In this regard, Cowie points out that in her "better works" Miss Woolson maintains her balance by preferring a "decent proportion to cheap intensity" (578).

5. Van Wyck Brooks, *Howells: His Life and World* (New York, 1959), p. 142.

6. For details concerning this letter, see above, Chapter I, note 29.

7. There is evidence in her notebooks to suggest that Miss Woolson was much more interested in this theme than her literary production would indicate. In at least five entries she jotted down ideas for characters or stories that deal with variations of it. See Benedict, II,

126, 127-28, 140-44, and 148-49. One can only regret that she did not manage to bring some of these ideas to fruition.

8. Nor, one might add, could she abide the saccharine romance and "too knightly" characterization of men in the fiction of many of her feminine contemporaries. For a candid airing of her views on these topics, see her letter of November 1, 1875, to Hayne.

9. On this point, see also Cowie, p. 574.

10. In his *Development of the American Short Story*, Pattee cites passages from "Rodman the Keeper" and "Felipa" to illustrate what he describes as "stiltedly bookish" talk (254-55).

Chapter Five

1. See J. Henry Harper, *The House of Harper*, pp. 484-85.

2. Even college students seldom study her work because it is now infrequently represented in anthologies of American literature. Until the 1930's her stories appeared in many collections, but of those that have been published in the last ten or fifteen years, her work has been represented in only one or two. Among these are Joe Lee Davis and others, eds., *American Literature: An Anthology and Critical Survey*, 2 vols., New York, 1948-49, and Lyon N. Richardson and others, eds., *The Heritage of American Literature*, 2 vols., Boston, 1950-51. In anthologies that have appeared in the last five years, I have not found any of Miss Woolson's work.

3. There is some evidence to suggest that Miss Woolson may still have a general reading public. In response to the distribution of the three volumes of her *Five Generations* in the 1930's, Miss Benedict received many letters both from those who received the books (chiefly librarians) and from those who read them. From these letters she made a selection that she had privately printed in England in 1941. The result was *Appreciations*. Quite a few of these letters are, of course, about Miss Woolson's literary productions; they reveal that as late as the 1930's a small body of readers in this country and Europe still knew and loved her work.

4. This situation is about to be corrected. Plans are now afoot for a volume of selections from Miss Woolson's fiction to appear in Twayne's United States Classics Series.

5. See, for instance, John Hervey, "Sympathetic Art" [a letter to the editor], *Saturday Review of Literature*, VI (October 12, 1929), 268; Kern, p. 176; Quinn, pp. 336-37; and Cowie, pp. 571-73.

Selected Bibliography

PRIMARY SOURCES

Books alone are listed here; all were published by Harper and Brothers except as indicated. For other works, the reader is referred to the entries under Benedict and Kern below.

The Old Stone House. Boston: D. Lothrop & Company, 1872. Published under the pseudonym of Anne March.

Castle Nowhere: Lake-Country Sketches. Boston: J. R. Osgood and Company, 1875; Harper after 1886.

Two Women, 1862. New York: D. Appleton and Company, 1877. Reprinted from *Appletons' Journal,* January and February, 1877.

Rodman the Keeper: Southern Sketches. New York: D. Appleton and Company, 1880; Harper after 1886.

Anne. 1882. Also in London: Sampson Low & Company, 1883.

For the Major. 1883. Also in London: Sampson Low & Company, 1883.

East Angels. 1886. Also in London: Sampson Low & Company, 1886.

Jupiter Lights. 1889. Also in London: Sampson Low & Company, 1889.

Horace Chase. 1894. Also in London: Osgood, McIlvaine & Company, 1894.

The Front Yard and Other Italian Stories. 1895.

Dorothy and Other Italian Stories. 1896 [c. 1895].

Mentone, Cairo, and Corfu. 1896 [c. 1895].

SECONDARY SOURCES

This list consists chiefly of books and articles containing information which relates directly to Miss Woolson or her work. Reviews of her fiction, manuscripts, letters, and other materials have been cited in the text and the footnotes.

ALDEN, HENRY MILLS. "Constance Fenimore Woolson," *Harper's Weekly,* XXXVIII (February 3, 1894), 113-14. Contains valuable information concerning the last months of CFW's life.

BENEDICT, CLARE (ed.). *Five Generations (1785-1923)*. 3 vols. London: Ellis [1929-1930]. This work is indispensable to the student of CFW. The second volume in particular, *Constance Fenimore*

Woolson (1930), contains materials found nowhere else. It was reprinted in 1932 with additions and a useful though incomplete bibliography of CFW's work.

———. *Appreciations. Leatherhead,* Surrey: F. B. Benger, 1941. A compilation of excerpts from letters received by Miss Benedict in response to her distribution of copies of *Five Generations* to libraries in America and Europe.

BROOKS, VAN WYCK. *The Times of Melville and Whitman.* New York: E. P. Dutton & Co., Inc., 1947. Deals perceptively with CFW's writings about the South.

COWIE, ALEXANDER. *The Rise of the American Novel.* New York: American Book Company, 1948. One of the best recent treatments of CFW's long fiction, including *For the Major.*

HUBBELL, JAY B. (ed.). "Some New Letters of Constance Fenimore Woolson," *New England Quarterly,* XIV (December, 1941), 715-35. A valuable article on CFW's views regarding the South; based on fifteen letters she wrote Paul Hamilton Hayne while she was living in the South in the late 1870's.

———. *The South in American Literature, 1607-1900.* Durham: Duke University Press, 1954. Contains an excellent brief discussion of CFW's fiction dealing with the South and a bibliographical note concerning this phase of her work.

JAMES, HENRY. "Miss Constance Fenimore Woolson," *Harper's Weekly,* XXXI (February 12, 1887), 114-15. Reprinted in *Partial Portraits.* London and New York: Macmillan and Co., 1888. May now be found in the *American Essays of Henry James,* ed. Leon Edel. New York: Vintage Books, 1956. Still the best essay on CFW's fiction; for obvious reasons, however, it contains no discussion of her work after *East Angels* (1886).

KERN, JOHN DWIGHT. *Constance Fenimore Woolson: Literary Pioneer.* Philadelphia: University of Pennsylvania Press, 1934. The only full-length scholarly treatment of CFW's life and work to date, it deals adequately with CFW's contributions to local-color fiction and less effectively with her other pioneer work: international-episode stories and the novel of analysis. The bibliography (especially of CFW's own work) is full and reliable.

MOORE, RAYBURN S. "Southern Writers and Northern Literary Magazines, 1865-1890." Unpublished dissertation (Duke University, 1956). Deals chiefly with CFW's writings about the South in *Harper's,* the *Atlantic, Lippincott's, Scribner's Monthly,* and the *Century.*

PATTEE, FRED LEWIS. *The Development of the American Short Story: An Historical Survey.* New York: Harper & Brothers, 1923. Treats

CFW as primarily a local colorist in her short fiction but points out her contribution to "more careful short-story workmanship."

———. "Constance Fenimore Woolson and the South," *South Atlantic Quarterly*, XXXVIII (April, 1939), 130-41. A revision of an address delivered by the author at the Dedicatory Exercises of the Constance Fenimore Woolson House at Rollins College, Winter Park, Florida, May 31, 1938, this article contains valuable information and offers one or two points beyond the scope of the title.

QUINN, ARTHUR HOBSON. *American Fiction: An Historical and Critical Survey*. New York: D. Appleton-Century Company, 1936. Students' edition. Deals sympathetically with both stories and novels and stresses the "artistic quality" of CFW's work.

RICHARDSON, LYON N. "Constance Fenimore Woolson, 'Novelist Laureate' of America," *South Atlantic Quarterly*, XXXIX (January, 1940), 18-36. Contains new biographical information and offers fresh critical insight into CFW's fiction. Based in part on letters written by CFW to her nephew Samuel Mather.

WAGENKNECHT, EDWARD. *Cavalcade of the American Novel*. New York: Henry Holt and Company, 1952. Discusses CFW's novels briefly and, for the most part, favorably.

Index

Index